Changing Military Patterns
of the Great Plains Indians

FRANK RAYMOND SECOY

CHANGING MILITARY PATTERNS OF THE GREAT PLAINS INDIANS

(17th Century through Early 19th Century)

Introduction to the Bison Book Edition by John C. Ewers

University of Nebraska Press
Lincoln and London

First published, 1953
Introduction copyright © 1992 by Frank Raymond Secoy
Manufactured in the United States of America

First Bison Book printing: 1992
Most recent printing indicated by the last digit below:
10   9   8   7   6   5   4   3   2   1

Library of Congress Cataloging-in-Publication Data
Secoy, Frank Raymond, 1922–
Changing military patterns of the Great Plains Indians (17th century through
early 19th century) / Frank Raymond Secoy: introduction to the Bison book edi-
tion by John C. Ewers.
p.   cm.
Originally published: Changing military patterns on the Great Plains (17th
century through early 19th century). Seattle: University of Washington Press,
1953, in series: Monographs of the American Ethnological Society; 21.
Includes bibliographical references.
ISBN 0-8032-9209-0
1. Indians of North America—Great Plains—Wars.   2. Indian warfare.   I.
Secoy, Frank Raymond, 1922–   Changing military patterns on the Great
Plains (17th century through early 19th century).   II. Title.
E78.G73S433   1993
978—dc20
92-16807   CIP

Reprinted by arrangement with the University of Washington Press. Originally published in 1953 as Monograph 21 of the American Ethnological Society.

ACKNOWLEDGMENTS

While studying at Columbia University my interest in the Great Plains was notably stimulated in class and seminar by Professor Wm. Duncan Strong. His dynamic view of the culture history of the Plains formed the basic framework within which the present study took shape. A long time has elapsed since the original problem and hypotheses which have controlled the organization of the investigation occurred to me. During this period a number of people have helped in various ways toward the development and completion of the work. Thus, I take this occasion to thank Professors Wm. Duncan Strong, Alfred L. Kroeber, Julian H. Steward, and Charles Wagley, all of whom read the manuscript at various stages and made valuable suggestions. Likewise, I thank William S. Willis, Helen Halley, Robert Stigler, Rosemary Spiro, Joseph Jablow, and Haldon Chase both for their constructive contributions and encouragement. Thanks are also due the Wenner-Gren Foundation for Anthropological Research for assistance in financing the publication of this monograph.

New York, N. Y.   Frank Raymond Secoy
January 1953.

TABLE OF CONTENTS

INTRODUCTION
By John C. Ewers

Most readers of western history tend to think of the Plains Indian wars in terms of those repeatedly described conflicts between war-bonneted Indians and uniformed soldiers of the United States that took place during the second half of the nineteenth century, rather than the prolonged intertribal encounters that date back to prehistoric times and continued until after the bison were exterminated on the plains.

Detailed accounts of the Indian-Soldier engagements at Sand Creek, the Washita, and the Little Big Horn have been told and retold in the popular literature on the American West. But few historians or anthropologists had attempted to survey and interpret the persistent warfare among the Indian tribes themselves before Frank Raymond Secoy, who studied in the libraries of New York City while he was a graduate student at Columbia University prior to 1951.

True, there had been occasional attempts to trace the history of individual tribes or groups of closely related ones in which the authors considered their relations with neighboring tribes. Indeed, as early as 1904 Doane Robinson, secretary of the South Dakota Department of History published a well-researched *History of the Dakota Sioux Indians* in which he told of their fights with other tribes as the westernmost divisions of the Sioux pushed westward from present-day Minnesota clear across the Dakotas to the valleys of the Yellowstone and Platte rivers in Montana and Wyoming during historic times (Robinson, 1904). But only five hundred copies of Robinson's work were printed and the volume was not reprinted until 1974. Meanwhile, in 1937, another historian, George E. Hyde, published *Red Cloud's Folk: A History of the Oglala Sioux Indians,* which provided a more popular history of that tribe of Indian warriors tracing their movements and wars with other Indians as well as with white soldiers between 1650 and 1878 (Hyde, 1937).

When I was a fellow student in anthropology at the Yale University Graduate School during the early 1930's David Mandelbaum prepared himself for fieldwork among the Plains Cree in Canada by reading everything he could find on both the history and the culture of those Indians. His study of them appeared as one of the Anthropological Papers of the American Museum of Natural History in 1940. It combined information he obtained through readings with that he obtained from elderly

Indians to show how their culture had changed over the years since their movement out of the woodlands onto the plains to become nomadic buffalo hunters at war with their western neighbors and to become allies of their former enemies, the Assiniboines. In its extensive use of historical sources Mandelbaum's study differed markedly from the many monographs on Plains Indians published earlier by the American Museum of Natural History, which relied primarily upon the memories of elderly Indian informants for knowledge of tribal life in buffalo days.

I believe that, despite or possibly because of the economic depression, the decade of the 1930s was one of great ferment in Plains Indian studies, and in American Indian studies in general, out of which emerged a much greater awareness of the importance and possibilities of more fruitful historical studies of Indian cultures.

For one thing, students of contemporary Indian cultures were trying to find ways to define and describe significant changes they were observing in the field. Scudder Mekeel, only a few years my senior, and Yale's first Ph.D. in anthropology, found, while studying the conservative and isolated communities on Pine Ridge Reservation, that a stock-taking of their household possessions was helpful in ascertaining the degree of a family's acceptance of white men's values. If, for example, they owned an alarm clock, they appeared to be giving up the older notion of "Indian time."

Anthropologists were beginning to call such studies of cultural change "acculturation studies." In 1937 Melville J. Herskovits of Northwestern University defined acculturation as "those phenomena which result when groups of individuals having different cultures come into continuous first hand contact with subsequent changes in cultural patterns of either or both groups." Furthermore, he pointed out that in acculturation studies recourse to recorded history "is mandatory" (Herskovits, 1937, pp. 259–64).

During the turbulent thirties William Duncan Strong was also digging into the Plains Indian past at significant archaeological sites and leading the way to a new and better understanding of the antiquity of Indian occupation of the Great Plains and of the dynamics of Plains Indian cultural change in prehistoric as well as historic times. His seminal paper, *The Plains Culture Area in the Light of Archaeology,* which appeared in the *American Anthropologist* in 1933, revealed how recent excavations in the plains were rewriting the story of the occupation of the area, beginning with the ancient hunters of an extinct species of bison thousands of years ago, followed by the intrusion of horticultural people from east of the Mississippi about the beginning of the Christian era and their movements up the major river valleys to become the dominant people of the region, until acquisition of the European horse enabled the nomadic tribes of the high plains to regain the ascendancy within the historic period and little more than a century before bison were exterminated and the tribes settled upon reservations (Strong, 1937).

Dr. Strong was teaching in the Department of Anthropology while Frank Raymond Secoy was a graduate student there, and Secoy gratefully acknowledged his indebtedness to Strong on the very first page of the published version of his 1951 dissertation. "My interest in the Great Plains was notably stimulated in class and seminar by Professor Wm. Duncan Strong. His dynamic view of the culture history of the Plains formed the basic framework within which the present study took shape."

Limited funds for ethnological fieldwork available at Columbia at that time may also have encouraged Secoy to select a topic for his dissertation that could be researched in the libraries of New York City. As the title of his dissertation indicated—"A Functional-Historical View of Plains Indian Warfare: The Process of Change from the 17th to the Early 19th Century"—Secoy was interested in cultural dynamics within a particular aspect of Plains Indian culture—warfare. He was also interested in acculturation, in the effects of white contacts upon the tactics employed in Plains Indian warfare.

He recognized that two major items introduced into Plains Indian culture from Europeans significantly changed these Indians' conduct of intertribal warfare—the horse and the gun. And he found that because it was Spanish policy to prohibit the sale or gift of firearms to Indians, these two items came to be received from opposite directions and from Europeans of different nations. The horse coming from the Spanish in the South and West; the gun from the French, English, and eventually Americans in the North and East. So Secoy sought to trace the advance of the horse frontier northward and eastward over the Great Plains; and of the gun frontier westward and southward from the eastern Woodlands, and to ferret out examples in the historical literature of the times to show how acquisition of the horse, on the one hand, and the gun, on the other, altered Plains Indian military tactics until after the tribes of the region obtained the advantages of both guns and horses.

The author found a few examples suggesting that prior to the Plains tribes' acquisition of either horses or guns they employed a military tactic of confronting each other with massed infantry in line formation, and armed with bow and arrows, lances, and clubs. Warriors also wore leather body armor made of several thicknesses of skin, and carried large shields of such size that they could hide behind them. Apparently there were few casualties in this pedestrian warfare unless one side so greatly outnumbered the other that it could encircle it and advance upon it from all directions. For a time tribes who adopted horses also adopted the Spanish custom of covering their horses with armor, using several layers of hides for this purpose, but thus depriving themselves of much of the mobility that horses offered them.

Meanwhile, Indians living on the northeastern plains began to acquire firearms as the white man's fur trade expanded westward. Indeed some of them obtained a few guns through Indian intermediaries even before they met white men. They soon learned that the increased firepower gave them a psychological as well as a material advantage over tribes farther west who fought only with bows and arrows and shock weapons. Gunless Indians feared those who possessed weapons that could launch a missile so fast that it could not be seen in flight and so powerful that it could penetrate a hide shield and kill its holder. Even after tribes learned to use guns they still looked upon them as endowed with supernatural power, as is indicated by the Sioux term for gun, which translates "sacred iron."

So Secoy continued to describe and to map the extension of both the horse and the gun frontier until after they intersected in the North and all the plains tribes secured the mobility of the horse and the deadly fire power of the gun, resulting in both an increase in the number of engagements and of casualties as well.

In his review of Dr. Secoy's monograph for the *American Anthropologist* William W. Newcomb declared it "a welcome addition to the growing body of literature which deals with Plains cultures by an historic and developmental method." He accepted Secoy's basic contention that the horse and gun were critical factors in the development of military tactics among those Indians during the portion of the historic period covered by Secoy's study. However, four years earlier in a carefully reasoned paper published in the *American Anthropologist* Dr. Newcomb had strongly advocated economic motives for Plains Indian warfare as opposed to the desires of individuals to win war honors. So he could not accept one statement in Secoy's work that appeared to recognize desire for revenge and personal prestige as ever-present motives for Sioux attacks upon the horticultural tribes of the Upper Missouri. Even so, Newcomb concluded: "With this small but significant exception, this study is a distinct contribution to the literature of the Plains Indian" (Newcomb, 1954, p. 304).

Since Secoy's monograph was published in 1953 a number of studies have appeared that have tended to revise or to expand upon his findings. For example, Jack D. Forbes' research in the Spanish Archives revealed that horses were diffused northward from Mexico into Texas as well as New Mexico during the seventeenth century and at a more rapid rate than Secoy indicated on his map of the horse frontier prior to 1675 (see page 104 of this volume). Forbes found that "by 1680 the Indians of all of Texas and New Mexico were mounted . . . and horses were being spread to even more northerly regions by the Plains Apaches and Utes" (Forbes, 1959, p. 208).

Studies published since 1953 have also defined more precisely the network of intertribal trade through which horses passed northward from the Southwest to the tribes of the Middle Missouri and Northern Plains prior to 1800. My own paper, *The Indian Trade of the Upper Missouri before Lewis and Clark: An Interpretation* (1954) included a map showing the locations involved in this trade and indicated that the expanding frontier of the horse had met that of the gun at the Mandan and Hidatsa villages—which had been important centers of Indian trade on the Upper Missouri since prehistoric times—by the 1740s. Certainly before Lewis and Clark's time it was customary for a horse to be traded for a gun at these centers.

Other scholars have continued the study of intertribal trade on the Great Plains and have tied it in with a vast network covering the entire American West. This larger picture has been presented best to date by William Swagerty in his essay "Indian Trade of the Trans-Mississippi West to 1870," which was published in Volume 4 of the Smithsonian's *Handbook of North American Indians* in 1988.

My own study, *The Horse in Blackfoot Indian Culture* (Ewers, 1955) was in press at the time Secoy's monograph appeared and I had no prior knowledge of Secoy's separate investigation. My study began in 1941 when I became the first curator of the Museum of the Plains Indian on the Blackfeet Reservation. It was based upon extensive interviews with elderly Piegan and Blood Indians, most of whom had participated in the last decades of intertribal warfare on the Northwestern Plains, as well as upon wide reading in the historical and anthropological literature on the Plains Indians.

My elderly informants made a clear distinction between two basic patterns of intertribal warfare—the revenge or scalp raid and the raid for horses. They differed markedly in organization and tactics as well as purpose. The very observant fur trader, Edwin T. Denig, who had known the tribes of the Upper Missouri since the early 1830s had recognized these same differences. In the mid-1850s he wrote succinctly: "War is made either to steal horses from their enemies or to take their scalps. For the first object but few people are required, as concealment and avoiding battle is aimed at and parties for this purpose are comprised of from 10 to 30 men, whereas a party starting expressly for battle often contains two, three, or four hundred warriors. . . . stealing horses is the most common kind of war excursions" (Denig, 1930, pp. 544ff).

David Thompson, who as a fur trader came to know the Blackfeet tribes as early as the 1790s, indicated that the Blackfeet recognized this difference when he wrote that the Piegan war chief, Kootenae Appe, "was utterly averse to small parties, except for horse stealing. . . . He seldom took the field with less than two hundred warriors but frequently with many more" (Thompson, 1916, p. 347).

My information indicated that scalp raiding was more common among the Blackfeet tribes and their enemies before 1855, although I was able to find descriptions of only eleven of them in my search of the literature on Blackfeet warfare during the first half of the nineteenth century. Even so, two of the greatest Blackfeet victories occurred as late as 1866 and 1870.

Secoy (on page 64 of this work) gives a rather detailed description of one of these actions in which the Piegans scored their most decisive victory in the memory of my informants. But Secoy's reference does not provide the motivation for the ferocity of the Piegan charge upon the combined force of Gros Ventres and Crows that caused the enemy to panic. That motivation was supplied by my Indian informants, who said that the Piegan warriors were enraged by the news that the enemy had killed their beloved head chief, Many Horses, which they received just before this battle. Whether this battle can be considered typical of post-horse and post-gun intertribal warfare as understood by Secoy is questionable.

The last large-scale battle in which the Blackfeet tribes participated occurred outside a trading post near present Lethbridge, Alberta, in the fall of 1870. Hoping to take advantage of a band of Blood Indians when they were intoxicated by the liquor they received from the traders, a large party of Cree Indians attacked at daybreak. But a number of Piegans who were in the vicinity came to the rescue. The Piegans were armed with repeating rifles while the Crees had only single-shot guns so they were able to kill more than two hundred of the enemy before they could get away (Ewers, 1955, pp. 194ff). One of my informants took part in that battle. But none of the others had participated in a large-scale intertribal action.

Whereas the large-scale raid involved elaborate preliminary ceremonies prior to departure, and the warriors rode or led their highly trained war ponies, carried shields, and elaborate war costumes, and there were post-raid scalp dances if the parties returned successfully, the horse raid was quite different. It required only a leader and a few followers, generally proceeded toward the enemy afoot, hiding out at night as it approached enemy territory, stealthily entering the enemy camp at daybreak, and removing as many of the best horses that were tethered near the doors of their lodges as possible before the enemy became aware of their action, and then making a quick getaway on the horses they had captured.

Even so, my studies showed there was a considerable degree of orga-

nization in those small war parties and that in this respect they resem-
bled quite closely the slave raids conducted by the pedestrian Illinois
against Plains Indians farther west about 1700, as described in detail in
the memoir of De Gannes concerning the Illinois country at that period
(Pease and Werner, 1934).

I also learned that my informants agreed with statements by nine-
teenth-century army officers who came to know the Plains Indians that
the nomadic tribes usually went to sleep at night without posting
guards, unless they had reason to believe that a raid on their horses was
imminent. This certainly helped to account for the high degree of success achieved by Blackfeet horse raiders.

Although it is improbable that any tribe of Plains Indians gained its
first horses by raiding, the horse raid must have gone back to but a brief
period after each tribe first received horses as gifts or in trade, and it persisted on the northern plains until after the nomadic tribes were placed
upon reservations. So the horse itself may be said to have been an important factor in perpetuating Plains Indian warfare.

Secoy's monograph has served archaeologists who have been studying the rock art of the northwestern plains in helping to determine the
relative ages of the petroglyphs and pistographs found in that region. In
The Plains War Complex and the Rock Art of Writing on Stone the ar-
chaeologist James D. Keyser cites Secoy as an influential source in his
studies of the rock art at that important site on the Milk River just north
of the international line in Alberta. There Indians appear to have por-
trayed intertribal warfare since prehistoric times. Incised representa-
tions of individual warriors standing and facing front with their upper
legs and bodies covered by large shields appear to have been the works of
prehistoric, pedestrian hunters. A representation of an Indian mounted
on a horse covered with armor, lancing an enemy on foot carrying one of
those large shields seems to date from the period of transition when one
side had horses and the other did not. Numerous other figures picturing
Indians on horseback and armed with guns must have been executed by
Indians of the more recent period when Indians possessed both horses
and guns (Keyser, 1979).

Historians also have continued to read and to be influenced by Dr.
Secoy's monograph. The most recent book on Plains Indian warfare to
come to my attention bears the title *Counting Coup and Cutting Horses:
Intertribal Warfare on the Northern Plains, 1738–1889.* Anthony Mc-
Ginnis, its author, offered this work as a doctoral dissertation at the
University of Colorado under the guidance of the late Robert G.
Athearn, a highly esteemed western historian. He acknowledged
Secoy's monograph as one of his sources (McGinnis, 1990).

Looking back upon Frank Raymond Secoy's monograph after a passage of four decades I think we should recognize it not only for its contribution to Plains Indian studies, but also to a method of researching the history and customs of a people that both historians and anthropologists now respect and know by the name of ethnohistory.

REFERENCES CITED

Ewers, John C.
1954 The Indian Trade of the Upper Missouri before Lewis and Clark: An Interpretation. *Bulletin Missouri Historical Society.* Vol. 10, pp. 429–46.
1955 The Horse in Blackfoot Indian Culture, with comparative material from other western tribes. *Bureau of American Ethnology Bulletin.* No. 159. Washington, D.C.
Denig, Edwin T.
1930 Indian Tribes of the Upper Missouri. Ed. by J. N. B. Hewitt. *46th Annual Report Bureau of American Ethnology,* pp. 375–626. Washington, D.C.
Forbes, Jack D.
1959 The appearance of the mounted Indian in Northern Mexico and the Southwest. *Southwestern Journal of Anthropology.* Vol. 15. No. 2, pp. 189–212.
Herskovits, Melville J.
1937 The Significance of the Study of Acculturation for Anthropology. *American Anthropologist,* Vol. 39, pp. 259–64.
Hyde, George E.
1937 *Red Cloud's Folk: A History of the Oglala Sioux Indians.* Norman. University of Oklahoma Press.
Keyser, James D.
1979 The Plains Indian War Complex and the Rock Art of Writing-on-Stone, Alberta, Canada. *Journal of Field Archaeology.* Vol. 6. No. 1 pp. 41–48.
Mandelbaum, David G.
1940 *The Plains Cree.* American Museum of Natural History. Anthropological Papers. Vol. 37, Pt. 2, New York.
McGinnis, Anthony
1990 *Counting Coup and Cutting Horses: Intertribal Warfare on the Northern Plains, 1738–1889.* Evergreen, Colorado. Cordillera Press, Inc.
Newcomb, William W.
1950 A Re-examination of the Causes of Plains Indian Warfare. *American Anthropologist.* Vol. 52, pp. 317–30.
1954 Review of Changing Military Patterns on the Great Plains by Frank Raymond Secoy. *American Anthropologist.* Vol. 56, p. 304.
Pease, T. C. and Werner, R. C., Editors
1934 Memoir of De Gannes concerning the Illinois Country. Collections Illinois State Historical Library. Vol. 23. French Series No. 1. Springfield, Illinois.
Robinson, Doane
1904 *A History of the Dakota or Sioux Indians.* South Historical Collections, Vol. 2, pp. 1–523.

Secoy, Frank Raymond
    1951   A functional-historical view of Plains Indian warfare: the process of
           change from the 17th to the early 19th century. Doctoral disserta-
           tion. Columbia University, New York.
Strong, William Duncan
    1933   The Plains Culture Area in the Light of Archaeology. *American An-
           thropologist*. Vol. 35, pp. 271–87.
Swagerty, William
    1988   *Indian Trade of the Trans-Mississippi West to 1870. History of In-
           dian-White Relations*. Ed. by Wilcomb E. Washburn. Handbook of
           North American Indians. Vol. 4, pp. 351–74. Washington, D.C.
Thompson, David
    1916   *David Thompson's Narrative of his Explorations of Western America,
           1784–1812*. Edited by J. B. Tyrrell Champlain Society Publication.
           No. 12. Toronto.

CHAPTER ONE

CULTURE, ENVIRONMENT AND THE DEVELOPMENT OF PLAINS MILITARY PATTERNS

The aim of this study is to show each of the various military technique patterns of the Indians of the Great Plains as a resultant of specific conditioning factors developing in time depth. In so far as the data permit, the influences and effects of each such pattern are traced both within a specific socio-cultural system and beyond it. The time limit for the beginning has been imposed by the period of the earliest adequate documentary sources for the area. The span of two centuries (approximately 1630–1830) covers all major changes in the military technique patterns in the Plains from the aboriginal phase to the full establishment of the pattern named in this study, the Horse *and* Gun pattern. A termination in the early 19th century is chosen, since this latter pattern persisted with only very minor changes throughout the middle and late 19th century until the military collapse of the native cultures. Furthermore, the remainder of the century has had by far the most intensive study, and is thus already well known.

From the point of view of a developmental study of Plains military technique patterns, three separate geographic areas, each having a unique combination of historical, environmental, and cultural factors, may be demarcated. These areas are as follows:

1. The southern subarea, including all of the Plains south of the North Platte and Platte Rivers.

2. The northwestern subarea, including all of the Plains west and north of a line running from the most easterly range of the Rocky Mountains, in the vicinity of Cheyenne, Wyoming, northeast across the North Platte River, north to the Black Hills, and due north from there to the northern margin of the Plains.

3. The northeastern subarea, including all of the Plains to the north of the North Platte and Platte Rivers, and to the east of the previously mentioned line through the Black Hills.

In addition, the Plains is divided into two natural areas, approximately demarcated by the 100th meridian. On the west is the High or Short Grass Plains, a region of scanty rainfall, averaging less than 20 inches a year, with altitudes ranging up to a mile or more above sea level. East of the 100th meridian is the Prairie or Tall Grass Plains, with a relative abundance of rainfall and elevations under 1000 feet above sea level.

1

The eastern regions of the Prairie Plains, the so-called "Eastern Borderlands" or "Margins," form a transition region between the Tall Grass Plains and the Eastern Deciduous Forest.

In the period studied here, two areas influenced by Europe bordered on the Plains. Adjoining the southern subarea on the southwest was the region controlled by Spain; to the north and east of the Great Plains was the region dominated by the French and the English. Each of the European colonial powers introduced a different complex of institutions and culture traits into its territory.

English and French Tradition versus Spanish Tradition

The geographic arrangement of these two different cultural traditions and environmental areas adjacent to opposite margins of the Plains area insured that two distinct influences would affect two separate marginal areas of the Plains. Each influence operated for some length of time independently of the other, and even after their fusion elsewhere on the Plains, each continued to exert a greater effect on the territory nearest its source. Each influence modified the original culture patterns of the territory it affected. The modified culture patterns were nevertheless still completely adapted to the special Plains environment and were therefore able to spread from their areas of origin throughout the entire Plains.

Of the many types of culture patterns which it would be possible to study within this polarized geographic framework, our attention is focused on the military technique patterns. In the development of these patterns the culture traits of crucial importance were the horse and the gun. During most of the period here dealt with, nearly the entire supply of horses and guns for the Great Plains flowed in from sources located on opposite sides of the area. Hence, there arose two distinct and opposed gradients in horse and gun distribution on the Plains. Within the separate geographic areas and under the organizing influence of these gradients, two distinct military technique patterns arose. The Post-horse—Pre-gun pattern of the southwest expanded to north and east with the advance of the Horse Frontier, while the Post-gun—Pre-horse pattern of the north and east expanded in opposite directions with the advance of the Gun Frontier. When the Horse Frontier and Gun Frontier met and overlapped, a new military technique pattern developed in the regions of intersection. This was the Horse *and* Gun pattern characteristic of the so-called "Typical" period of Plains Indian culture. This pattern, in its turn, spread in all directions to the margins of the Plains.

The factors determining the locus of origin of the Horse Frontier were mainly environmental. The forested area adjacent to the Plains on the northeast and north, from whence came the first strong European influences on the adjoining section of the Plains, was quite unsuited to the natural growth and multiplication of horse herds, or to the use of the horse for transportation to any considerable degree. This being the case, horses were not available for diffusion to the Plains from this region. On the other hand, the region bordering the Plains on the southwest, today comprising New Mexico, northern Mexico and coastal Texas, afforded plenty of good range land, ideal for horse breeding. In such extensive treeless areas the horse was also the best mode of transportation. For these reasons, the southwest was the first area to offer the horse to the Plains Indian, and it continued to supply most of the animals at any given period.[1] Thus a gradient in the supply of horses was formed, with a steadily decreasing concentration of the animals as the distance north and east of the source of supply in New Mexico increased.

The effects of differing cultural factors are most apparent in the case of the gun gradient. To explain why it was that guns diffused to the Plains Indians from the northern and eastern margins of the Plains, and not from the southwestern areas adjacent to the Plains, one must turn to a study of European history during this period. Differences between France and England, on the one hand, and Spain, on the other, led to markedly different policies of overseas expansion. Spanish overseas expansion was directly state-controlled and emphasized the conquest of areas and the subjugation of their inhabitants. Imperial policy accomplished the incorporation of conquered peoples into the state by means of political and religious institutions designed as instruments of control. The state regulated economic production and distribution by its conquered subjects.

In contrast to the Spanish imperial policy, the primary or frontier phase of the English and French expansion was only indirectly controlled by the state and emphasized exploitation for immediate profit by individuals or joint stock companies.[2] In the context of the natural and human resources of northeastern North America this attitude led to the development of the fur trade as the major type of contact relationship between European and Indian. Because this was a trade relationship, and because competition existed among individual traders, particularly between French and English traders, it was possible for the Indian to satisfy any need which he could transform into an effective economic demand by acquiring furs for trading purposes. The Indian

---

[1] Regarding the lack of significant horse-raising among the Plains Indians (see Haines, Francis, 1938a, pp. 113–114). Moreover, when Bourgmont was among the Paduca in 1724, he discovered that "...they never raise colts, for the mares all have miscarriages in the hunts." (Margry, 1879–88, vol. 6, pp. 444–45; see also Mishkin, 1940, p. 6).

[2] MacLeod, 1928, chapters 6, 11, 12, 13, 14.

greatly needed guns and ammunition. Since both Indians and traders found their trade relationship advantageous, the traders did not consider the possession of guns by Indians beyond the frontier a threat to themselves. The only exception was the case in which the Indians who were equipped with guns were connected through trade relations with the fur trade system of a competing national group. Such Indians could be very dangerous, the prime example of this danger being the Iroquois, who were linked by trade first with the Dutch and later with the English, and who therefore constituted a long continued threat to New France. However, from the European point of view, such unpleasant situations were not inherent in the relations arising out of the fur trade itself, but resulted from the accident of intense rivalry between nations at a particular time and place.

In the Spanish area, where emphasis was not upon trade across the frontier to acquire wealth, but upon controlled production and distribution of wealth within the empire, the possession of guns by Indians beyond the frontier was a severe threat to the maintenance of the frontier and to its future advance. For that reason, the sale of guns and ammunition to Indians beyond the frontier was forbidden by law.[3] There

[3] The following evidence confirms this legal prohibition:
a) Worcester, 1944, p. 2.
b) Bolton, 1915, p. 116.
c) In 1724, the Paduca (i. e. the Apache) told Bourgmont that the Spaniards, "... trade us only knives and bad axes, but they are not as you who give us guns ..." Margry, 1879–88, vol. 6, p. 449.
d) One of the greatest worries the Spaniards had about the French was that they would supply the Indians, especially the Caddoans, with guns. (See Thomas, 1935, pp. 4,-31, 36, 131, 144).
e) A local reaffirmation of the law, sometime between 1731 and 1736, by a governor of New Mexico: "An order was issued by this governor prohibiting the sale of arms to the tribes of the Plains or foreigners under heavy penalties... a fine of 10,000 maravedis for Spaniards, and one hundred lashes and fifty days imprisonment for Indians." (Haines, Helen, 1891, p. 115).
f) MacLeod, 1928, p. 319.
g) A statement of traditional Spanish policy, unchanged as late as 1772, in a letter of the Fiscal to the Viceroy of Mexico: "The Fiscal does not think that these proposals of the Baron de Riperda [he had proposed trading "... guns, ammunition, and hunting knives to the Indians of the North, neighbors of our frontiers and of the English and French..." FRS] ... conform to the maxims, principles, and rules of a defensive war, or of a conquest like that which occupies the attention of our interior presidios and of the missions which they guard, when there may be other means by which our purposes would succeed without such risk, and without the disadvantages of giving arms to the enemy and wishing to overcome their power, which is the whole object of the Governor's opinion." (Bolton, 1914, pp. 278–79, 88–89, 97).
h) The basic legal sanction is in the following law which was frequently reaffirmed in the course of time: "Ley XXXI. Que no se pueden vendar armas a los Indios, ne ellos las tengan. D. Fernando V, y Doña Isabel en Granada a 17 de Septiembre de 1501. El Emperador D. Carlos a 16 de Febrero de 1536.

is abundant continuous evidence in the documentary sources that this law was quite effectively enforced by the local administrations until the first quarter of the 19th century. Hence, almost all of the guns possessed by any of the Plains tribes prior to the 19th century were obtained largely through trading with the English and French on the north and east. The supply of the lead and powder necessary for continued operation of these guns was obtained in a similar fashion.

The existence of horse and gun gradients, in the early period, in the form of a decline in the number of horses locally available as the distance increased from southwest to north and east, as well as a decline in the number of guns at an increasing distance from north and east to southwest, had a vital effect on the military technique pattern of tribes located at different points along these gradients. In the next chapter, the fate of the groups of Plains Indians located nearest the origin of the horse gradient will be considered.

y el Principe Gobernador en Madrid a 17 de Diciembre de 1551. D. Felipe II a 25 de Enero de 1536. y a 10 de Diciembre de 1566. y a 18 de Febrero de 1567. y a 1 de Marzo de 1570. "We order and command that no one sell or distribute arms, offensive, or defensive, to the Indians, not to any of them; and whoever does the contrary, being Spaniard, for the first time, he pays 10,000 maravedis, and for the second time, he loses half of all his possessions to our Department and Treasury, and the corporal punishment will be at our mercy, from the said pecuniary penalties, the person who accused takes the fourth part for himself, and the justice who passes sentence takes another fourth part; and if he were Indian, and was carrying sword, club, or daggar, or had other arms, they are to be taken away and be sold, and in addition be condemned to the same penalties that appear just, except some particular Indian to whom we may permit that he be granted license by the Viceroy, Audiencia, or Governor to carry them." (In "Recopilacion de Leyas de los Reynos de las Indias," 1943, Tomo II, Libro VI, Titulo I, p. 196).

CHAPTER TWO

POST-HORSE—PRE-GUN PATTERN ON THE SOUTHERN PLAINS

In the 17th century the Apache occupied the extreme Southwestern Plains. This group was geographically closest to the primary source of horses and was more directly under the influence of Spanish culture than were any of the other Plains tribes. The Apache appear to have developed the Post-horse—Pre-gun military technique pattern to its most elaborate state. Since they surrounded the settlements of New Mexico on the west, north, and east, they must have been the first to adopt the use of the horse, aside from the peoples of the Pueblos. In turn, the Apache appear to have transmitted the horse to the peoples to their east and north on the Plains, and, in conjunction with the Utes, to the north along the transmontane route.[1]

Apache

The subsistence pattern of the Pre-horse Plains Apache[2] is difficult to determine. It is easy to establish the fact that bison hunting was very important, but hard to ascertain whether horticulture was present or absent. The very early Spanish sources do not as a rule distinguish the Navaho Apache from the other Apache groups in a definite fashion. Thus, one reference to the Apache by Benavides[3] clearly alludes to the Navaho Apache, but sounds as if it were also intended to include the Plains Apache to the east of New Mexico. If this were so it would mean that not only the ancestral Navaho Apache but also the eastern or Plains Apache practiced some horticulture in addition to hunting in the Pre-horse period. However, other passages in the very early Spanish sources which clearly refer to the Plains Apache of that day mention only the nomadic life of food gathering and bison hunting, using dog

[1] See Haines, Francis, 1938*b* and Worcester, 1944, pp. 225–232, and especially pp. 226–27.
[2] From now on, this text will refer exclusively to the Plains Apache, unless otherwise indicated.
[3] Hodge, 1945. "In fact, the Apaches surround the above-mentioned nations [i. e., the Pueblos] on all sides and have continuous wars with them.:... The Apaches worship only the sun and the moon. They wear clothing, and although their chief sustenance is derived from hunting, they also plant much corn." (p. 81). "... all those fifty leagues from Xila up to this Navajo nation are settled with rancherias... The whole land is teeming with people." (p. 85).

transport.[4] This is strong evidence against the existence of horticulture among these people. However, the possibility is not ruled out that horticulture was practiced to some degree in summer in areas far removed from the Pueblos, while a nomadic hunting life occupied the rest of the year. Trade and other contact with the Pueblo Indians and the Spaniards of New Mexico would then have occurred only during the nomadic hunting phase of their annual economic cycle. If the hypothesis of a partial horticultural economy is correct, the adoption of the horse only intensified the pre-existing economy of the Plains Apache. However, if the more commonly accepted hypothesis of the absence of horticulture is correct, then the adoption of the horse, in some unexplained manner, made possible the addition of horticulture to a previously, purely hunting and gathering economy.

In any case, there is clear evidence that during the Post-horse period the Apache of the Plains were living a semi-sedentary — semi-nomadic life based on an annual cycle. They apparently chose favorable agricultural "rancherias" (*rancheria*, a Spanish word meaning "hut," but used in the New World to mean "hamlet" or "small village") which they occupied continuously from spring until the harvest in August. Of course, hunting and war parties took part of the manpower away at times during this period, but the remainder of the people were in continuous occupation until after the harvest. Then, the population of a number of rancherias came together into one band for the fall and winter buffalo hunt, equipped with hide tipis and horse transport, to lead a nomadic life until spring.[5]

At the beginning of the 18th century, when the Plains Apache occupied their most extensive area, their horticultural rancherias were to be found in favorable river valley sites throughout the territory of what is now eastern New Mexico and Colorado and western Nebraska,

[4] For example: "This nation [Apaches Vaqueros] extends for more than another hundred leagues to the east [of the Pueblos] and clothe themselves on the famous cibola cattle ... using the hides for clothing."

And the Pueblos said of the Plains Apache that "... they live on game and eat nothing except meat of the cattle during the winter ... during the rainy season they go in search of prickly pears and dates; ... they do not have houses only huts of cattle hides; ... they move from place to place; ... they were their enemies, but they also came to their Pueblos with articles of barter such as deer skins and cattle hides for making footwear, and with a large amount of meat in exchange for corn and blankets ..." (Hammond and Agapito, 1927, p. 91).

[5] As nomads, they were often encountered by European explorers. For example, the Valverde expedition in the fall of 1719 met part of the Plains Apache in eastern Colorado embarked on the hunting phase of their annual cycle.

"... the Apache horde of Cuartelejos, Palomas, and Calchufines arrived ... some 200 tipis, numbering in all, Valverde estimated, more than one thousand souls, warriors, women, and children." (Thomas, 1935, p. 31). A few years later, when considering the possibility of establishing a post at El Cuartelejo, the Spaniards note that: "... the Apache ... leave after harvesting their crops." (*Ibid.*, p. 34).

Kansas, Oklahoma and Texas.[6] Part of the documentary evidence for the existence of these horticultural settlements may be found in the accounts of the Ulibarri expedition of 1706. A four days' march northeast of the present site of Cimarron, New Mexico, the Spaniards met friendly Apaches, who were living "... in their rancherias, where as good people they cultivated grain, maize, corn, frijoles, and pumpkins..."[7] On their arrival at El Cuartelejo (either in eastern Colorado or western Kansas, more probably the latter) they noted the fertility of the soil "... that produced crops of maize, watermelons, pumpkins, wheat, and kidney beans..."[8] Here they were invited by the Apache to participate in a raid they had planned on the Pawnee and French,[9] in retaliation for a raid which these peoples had undertaken against El Cuartelejo when they had received information "... that the Apache braves were away hunting buffalo..."[10]

Further documentary evidence is provided by the records of the Hurtado expedition of 1715, undertaken against the Faraones Apache of eastern New Mexico. Their nearest settlement was "...ten days' marching to the east [i. e., of Santa Fe], where there were thirty wooden dwelling places on a river...." The Pueblo Indian informants of the Spaniards considered that"...the best time to campaign was about the middle of August, when the Faraones were reaping, for afterwards until the following April or May they hunted buffalo for hides, or Pueblos — for corn."[11] Later, when the Valverde expedition of 1719 against the Comanche arrived in the vicinity of El Cuartelejo, the commander was informed by a Paloma Apache that "... while he and his people were in his lands, which is farther in from El Cuartelejo, on the most remote borderlands of the Apaches, the French united with the Pawnees and Jumanos, attacked them from ambush while they were planting corn."[12]

This new combination of maize, buffalo, and the horse furnished a basis for the subsistence of an enlarged population; indeed, it is probable that within a few generations the Apache population increased considerably.[13] This increase, in turn, stimulated a drive toward expansion, which the horse, as transport, facilitated.

[6] *Ibid.*, p. 29; Margry, 1879–88, vol. 6, pp. 444–45.
[7] Thomas, 1935, p. 16.
[8] *Ibid.*, p. 21.
[9] *Ibid.*, p. 19.
[10] *Ibid.*, p. 20.
[11] *Ibid.*, p. 24.
[12] *Ibid.*, p. 131.
[13] Although this hypothesis of population growth is entirely inferential, it seems most probable. There is no evidence to the contrary. Moreover, a survey of Plains population trends in the 18th and 19th centuries (see Rands, 1950, "Chart of Plains Populations," MS) reveals an astonishing vitality among the nomadic, bison hunting groups. This was a phase of greatly increased white contact and pressure as compared with the 17th and very early 18th centuries. Yet, even under

The Apache expansion developed on a front of about 180⁰, from nearly north, through east, to south. This expansion brought the Apache into continual conflict with the tribes of the Eastern and Southern Plains borderlands. As a result of the demands made by these hostilities, the Apache evolved a new military pattern, horse warfare, which was designed, in this early period, to overcome enemies using the older Pre-horse military pattern. The new pattern was based on the possession of large numbers of horses, and required access to a supply for continual replenishment. The new pattern also implied heavy borrowing of culture elements from the Spaniards and the Pueblo Indians of New Mexico.

Apache expansion did not take place on a 360⁰ front, because of the lack of a proper environment for their new economic cycle in some of the adjacent regions. The barrier of the Rocky Mountains stretched to the north and west from New Mexico, while to the south and west the land lacked the buffalo. In addition, New Mexico itself was occupied by the militarily strong Pueblo Indians and Spaniards. However, the region to the north, on the east side of the Rockies (the High Plains), was excellent open buffalo country and only sparsely populated, if at all, by nomadic hunters using foot and dog transport.[14] Such a population could be assimilated or eliminated without much difficulty. But beyond the High Plains, to the northeast and southeast of New Mexico, were the relatively dense populations of the horticultural Caddoan peoples.

The more Plainsward of these groups occupied a transitional area between the Plains and the Prairie to north and east (the Caddoans of Nebraska), and between the Plains and the Southeastern Woodland area to east and south (the Caddoans of Oklahoma and Texas). This transitional belt provided opportunity for bison hunting in the grasslands and horticulture in the many suitable stream valleys. Apparently, the resident Caddoans exploited both of these aspects of the environment, although they concentrated on horticulture and the sedentary village life. For them, buffalo hunting was a seasonal affair of brief expeditions on foot, assisted by dog transport. In illustration of this type of economic adjustment on the eastern margins of the Plains we note that even at a somewhat later period, in 1724, Bourgmont found the horticultural Kansa on a short summer bison hunt somewhere in eastern Kansas. The women and dogs carried all the baggage while the

these conditions the nomadic groups either held their own up until the extinction of the bison, or decreased only slightly. When we understand that there were severe epidemics in 1778, 1781–82, 1801, 1837 and 1849, it is clear that mere maintenance of the population level, on a long term basis, implied a very rapid population increase after each epidemic. Hence, there seems no reason to doubt that the much more favorable situation of the Apache in the 17th century led to a rapid increase in population.

[14] Kroeber, 1947, p. 78.

men formed an escort and engaged in hunting. These Kansa were eager for a peace with the Paduca (Apache) so that they could acquire horses for transport.[15]

It is apparent that this transitional belt would have been particularly attractive to the Apache, since it offered full opportunities for exploitation by their annual subsistence cycle which was rather evenly divided into nomadic hunting and sedentary horticultural phases. Thus, impelled by population growth and drawn by a region especially favorable for exploitation by their new economic pattern, the Apache came into conflict with the borderland Caddoans over the possession of the land of the latter. The new pattern of Apache warfare grew out of this prolonged struggle.

Caddoans

The Pre-horse—Pre-gun military technique pattern of the horticultural Caddoans apparently consisted of battles between massed infantry forces and put a premium on numerical strength. Firepower with the bow was heavily stressed, supplemented by shock with the spear and, especially, the war club. There appears to have been little use of the shield and no body armor.[16] The warriors were organized in squadrons of up to about 100 men in size. When the concept of a formal battle was put into operation the two enemy forces drew themselves up in a parallel line formation, sometimes with both ends of the line thrown forward, making a concave arc. It is apparent that when such formations are opposed on a battlefield the advantage, other things being equal, lies with the line that is deeper and, even more important, longer. At the point where the longer line overlaps the shorter, the latter is exposed to being partially surrounded and progressively crushed by the resulting superior concentration of manpower in this crucial region. Hence, in this type of battle, sheer manpower is a great military asset, for the larger the number of men that can be assembled on the battlefield, the greater the probability of victory. It therefore follows that the techniques of food production which can support the denser population give a military advantage to the group that uses them. Likewise, organizational techniques which bring warriors from a number of groups together for united action give an advantage to the participating groups. With

[15] Margry, 1879–88, vol. 6, pp. 413–415. For a discussion of the identity of the "Paduca" cf. Secoy, 1951.

[16] I have found no reference to armor among the Caddoans west of the Mississippi in the earliest contact period. This also seems to be true for the whole southeastern culture area south of Virginia, of which the Caddoans of this period were a peripheral manifestation. Hough states: "I have not met with accounts of armor among the southern tribes, as the Muskoki group and others..." (Hough, 1895, pp. 649–50).

reference to the first point, horticulture supplemented by buffalo hunting gave the borderlands Caddoans a relatively dense population. With reference to the second point, they had developed the mechanism of loosely united confederations in which the war chief of one member group was given command over the temporarily assembled contingents of warriors. It is thus apparent that a group, such as the Pre-horse Apache, leading primarily a nomadic hunting life, would find it very difficult to invade successfully a well-populated region having this military technique pattern. Permanent occupation could be secured only by defeating the enemy through the employment of his own tactics. The manpower necessary to implement these tactics successfully would hardly ever be available to the nomad. Of course, the Post-horse—Pre-gun military technique pattern eventually solved the problem posed to the Apache by the Pre-horse—Pre-gun Caddoan pattern.

A more detailed description of the Pre-horse—Pre-gun Caddoan military technique pattern shows that there were sometimes variations on the "line" battle plan. One such variation took the form of an immediate encirclement of the enemy force, when it was considerably smaller than that of the attackers.

Another variation consisted in dividing the force and then making a succession of timed attacks. Several sections of the army would creep around the enemy and lie in hiding, waiting until the main force had fully engaged the entire enemy army before delivering an attack from the rear. Still another practice was to divide the force, usually into two bodies, and then make a simultaneous assault from different directions. Caddoan warfare is described in operation in the following quotations from early Spanish accounts of expeditions into the region between the Mississippi River and the true Plains.

The De Soto expedition of 1539–43 spent a number of months wandering about in southern Arkansas, southeastern Oklahoma, eastern Texas, and northern Louisiana, during which period there were numerous hostile encounters with the Caddoan inhabitants of the area. Once, when the Spaniards entered a village, the natives immediately counter-attacked.

> But no sooner did they know that he was in the town, than at four o'clock on the morning of the first night, they came upon him in two squadrons, from different directions, with bows and arrows and long staves like pikes.[17]

On another occasion, several Indian scouts from the enemy army were captured, and

> The prisoners being asked by the Governor why they had come, they said, to discover the numbers he had, and their condition, having been sent by their lord, the chief of Naguatex; and that he, with the other caciques, who came in

[17] Hodge, 1907, p. 219.

his company and his cause, had determined on giving him battle that day. While thus conferring, many Indians advanced, formed in two squadrons, who, so soon as they saw that they were descried, giving whoops, they assailed the Christians with great fury, each on a different quarter .... the greater part of the cavalry pursuing them, forgetful of the camp, when those that remained were attacked by another two squadrons, that had lain in concealment .... one of the Indians, brought back alive, being asked by the Governor who they were that had come to give them battle, said the cacique of Naguatex, the one of Maye, and another of a province called Hacanac, lord of great territories and numerous vassals, he of Naguatex being in command.[18]

It is possible, and indeed not unlikely, that the Pre-horse—Pre-gun Plains Apache may have had a military technique pattern essentially similar to the Caddoan one just described. This would be supported by fairly solid evidence if we could be sure that the Spaniards used the term "Escanjaques" as an alternative name for the Apache in the very earliest period. The evidence in favor of this interpretation is that Spanish explorers of the 16th century speak of the "Escanjaques" in the same Plains area to the east of the Pueblos that they say is inhabited by the "Apache Vaqueros." Likewise, their description of these people, and of their material culture and economy, corresponds to descriptions of the Plains Apache of that period. Shortly after the beginning of the 17th century the Spanish sources cease to refer to the "Escanjaques" and the only people described as inhabiting the Plains to the east are various groups of "Apache."

In 1601, the Oñate expedition crossed the Plains and began to enter the eastern borderlands in either eastern Kansas or Oklahoma. At this point they met a large camp of the nomadic "Escanjaques," equipped with skin tipis and large quantities of hides which they used for clothing. The Spaniards also stated that "They were not a people who sowed or reaped, but they lived solely on the cattle."[19] These people were at war with another group some distance to the east down a wide river lined with trees. The latter were horticulturalists living in a permanent village of round cane-walled houses with roofs of grass thatch.[20] Turning back to the west, the expedition encountered the now hostile "Escanjaques" and, in the words of the chronicler,

... those who most desired war began it with very great fury, presenting in their first stand more than fifteen hundred persons, who, placed in order in a semicircle, attacked with great valor and force ... the shower of arrows was great ... the Indians became more furious than at the beginning, keeping it up for more than two hours with the greatest courage ...[21]

Thus, if these "Escanjaques" were the Plains Apache, as they may well have been, the military technique pattern of battles with massed

18 *Ibid.*, p. 239.
19 Bolton, 1916, p. 257.
20 *Ibid.*, p. 260.
21 *Ibid.*, pp. 263–64.

infantry in line formation armed with bow, spear, and club was the Pre-horse—Pre-gun form on the Southern Plains. The fact that this appears to have been the Pre-horse—Pre-gun pattern on the North-western Plains is noted in Chapter III.

In the Post-horse—Pre-gun period the Apache military technique pattern assumed a quite different character. As a result of conflict with the borderlands Caddoans and contact with the Spaniards and Pueblo Indians of New Mexico, the Plains Apache had developed a pattern of mounted warfare utilizing the short bow and the saber-tipped lance for offense. For defense they had a small leather shield and used leather armor for both horse and rider.[22] The equipment of the Apache mounted warrior was relatively elaborate, and apparently modeled in considerable detail on that of the Spanish cavalryman. It included metal bit and stirrups, and the high pommeled, high cantled saddle necessary for the best use of the lance. It lacked only those items which could neither be purchased from New Mexico nor manufactured locally. The following quotations referring to the late 17th and early 18th centuries illustrate the war equipment of the Apache in use, and call attention to the use of leather armor:

With a force of one hundred and fifty seven Spaniards, sixty mission Indians and nine hundred horses and mules, Bustillo [in 1731] went by way of the San Xavier River to a stream which was apparently the San Saba. Here he encountered several hundred Indians of the Lipan and other Apache bands, protected by *leather breastplates.*[23]

During this period they [i. e., the Apache] apparently did not use firearms but fought on horseback, with bows, spears, and darts, and had *armor for both man and horse.*[24]

In his diary of 1691, Father Massanet made the following statement concerning the Apaches ..., ".... In the end they conquer all the tribes; yet it is said they are not brave because they fight with *armored horses.*[25] They have defensive and offensive weapons, and are very skilful and warlike Indians."[26]

The equipment of an Apache warrior, the witnesses tell us, was quite elaborate. They possessed many horses, had good saddles with iron stirrups, and used bridles. *Their horses were usually protected from the arrows of the enemy by buffalo skins, and the Apaches themselves used skin armor,*[27] painted variously blue, red, green, or white. No mention is made of the Apaches having firearms and it is made to appear that they fought entirely without them. Their arrows were generally tipped with iron, we are told, and they also used a kind of iron dart (chuza) in offensive warfare. Their clothing as a rule was of buckskin.[28]

When they [i. e., Paduca who were the Apache] go to war they always go on horses, and they have specially tanned buffalo skins with which they protect themselves, and with which they surround the horses to ward off arrows.[29]

[22] Dunn, W. E., 1910–1911, p. 206; French, 1851, vol. 3, pp. 47–48.
[23] Bolton, 1915, p. 28. Italics FRS.
[24] Dunn, W. E., 1910–1911, p. 203. Italics FRS.
[25] Italics FRS.
[26] Dunn, W. E., 1910–1911, p. 203.
[27] Italics FRS.
[28] Dunn, W. E., 1910–1911, p. 222.
[29] Margry, 1879–88, vol. 6, p. 445.

In addition to the foregoing evidence, there is a Ponca tradition about the Paduca (i. e., Apache), which relates that

> ... at that time the Ponca had no animals but dogs to help them to carry burdens .... While they were off hunting buffalo they first met the Padouca, and afterwards had many battles with them. The Padouca were mounted on strange animals .... The Padouca had bows made from elk horn. They were not very long .... To protect their horses from arrows they made a covering for the horses' breasts and sides. .... This covering ... was made of thick rawhide cut in round pieces and made to overlap like the scales of a fish. Over the surface was sand held on by glue. This covering made the Ponca arrows glance off and do no damage. The Padouca protected their own bodies by long shields of rawhide. Some of them had breastplates made like those on their horses.[30]

Spanish Armament Tradition

Curtis, our best source of information on the Spanish military equipment used in the Southwest,[31] tells us that the chief officers in the cavalry of the Coronado expedition, 1540–42, wore a battle dress of full plate armor covering them from head to foot, with the battle-helmet replaced, when not in action, by a broad hat reinforced by hidden steel bands. A cloak was used while on the march to protect the person from the effects of the sun shining on the steel armor. As arms they used lances, swords, daggers, and possibly the wheel-lock pistol and the wheel-lock carbine. The regular cavalryman probably wore a suit of three-quarter plate armor protecting the upper arms and the body from neck to knee with steel. Heavy leather boots and gauntlets completed the armor. Their helmet was the "salade" type. They were armed with lances, swords, daggers, and possibly pistols. The horses were protected by bardings, a long, loose drapery that hung from the saddle and harness, furnishing a partial protection against arrows and spears. Possibly the officers' horses were protected by leather or steel plates on forehead, chest, and croup. The arms of the infantry varied. Some had crossbows, some had muskets, and others had sword and shield. Still others had pike, halberd, bill, or poleax. The armor of the infantry probably consisted of two different types, one, typical of the European battlefield and consisting of a leather jerkin and a steel corselet from which hung a pair of tuilles, steel plates coming down nearly to the knee, the other, typical of the Aztec-Maya area and consisting of a coat of tightly quilted cotton covering the body to the middle of the thigh, and effective, to a large extent, not only against the piercing effect of arrows and lances, but also against the crushing blows of clubs and stone-hammers. The infantry helmets were the morion and the pikeman's pot.

---

[30] Fletcher and La Flesche, 1905–1906, p. 79.
[31] Curtis, 1927, pp. 107–33.

By the time of the first lasting conquest and occupation of New Mexico by Oñate at the beginning of the 17th century, the cavalry was armed with arquebuses, but otherwise unchanged from Coronado's period. The armor was also about the same, but more of the cavalry contented themselves with a salade helmet and a cuirass, or half suit of armor, supplemented by a leather jacket and tuilles.

By the period of the Pueblo Revolt and Reconquest, at the end of the 17th century, armor was rapidly disappearing from use in Europe, but was still surviving strongly in the Southwest. Governor Otermin attempted to remedy the shortage of regular armor immediately following the Revolt by making some from boiled ox-hides, an ancient practice which had been obsolete for years.[32] During this period in general, the cavalry wore the morion helmet, body armor ranging from the three-quarters suit to the cuirass alone, and heavy leather gauntlets and boots. They were armed with lance, sword, musket, and possibly, pistols. The infantry had cuirass, or leather jacket, and morion or reinforced hat. They were armed with pikes, halberds and muskets. Shields were still used by infantry and cavalry.

There was a general trend toward a replacement of the expensive metal armor bit by bit by leather. The trend began some time after the first occupation of New Mexico in the early 17th century and was imposed by the general poverty of the province. Such a replacement was possible because the weapons of the Indians had such a low penetrative power that leather could protect against them nearly as well as steel. From the accounts of the Reconquest of New Mexico by De Vargas, which began in 1692, it is apparent that at least the rank and file of the Spanish cavalry were armored exclusively in leather, except for their steel helmets. There is constant reference to "leather jackets," and to their vital importance, while there is very little reference to metal pieces of armor. According to Denhardt[33] this leather armor consisted of a long sleeveless leather jacket, for the rider, and an apron of leather, for the protection of the horse, which was hung around its chest and then tied to the saddle horn. Shield, lance, saber, and arquebus completed the soldier's equipment.

Such was the Spanish armament tradition with which the Apache came in contact, both directly during the early and middle 17th century, and indirectly, as assimilated by the Pueblo Indians, during the later period of the Revolt and Reconquest.

[32] *Ibid.*, p. 120.
[33] Denhardt, 1947, p. 116.

Native Armor Tradition

While it has been said that the armor of the mounted Indians of the Southwest was directly copied from the Spaniards,[34] the situation was not quite as simple as this. There was a native leather armor tradition in North America, as distinct from the Spanish leather armor tradition which was imported into the Southwest from Europe and underwent secondary development there. The aboriginal type differed slightly from area to area, but had a distinctive form and method of manufacture. These leather coats of armor ". . . were always made in one piece folded over, sewed above the shoulders, leaving an orifice for the head and with a hole cut out of the left side for the left arm, the right side of the garment remaining open. The skin was often doubled, but more frequently the coat was reinforced with pieces of thick hide. Sometimes shoulder guards were added."[35] Another distinctive method in its manufacture was that successive layers of leather were bound together by gluing.[36] Finally, there was a special technique for increasing the protective power of the armor by the use of one or more layers of sand, or sand and gravel, held on by glue. Sometimes the sand was mixed with the glue which held the layers of leather together, as in the case of the Shoshone armor recorded by Lewis and Clark,[37] and sometimes it was made into a final outer layer, as recorded of the 19th century Déné by Morice[38] and of the 17th century "Padouca," in the Ponca tradition by Fletcher and La Flesche.[39] Although this layer of sand technique was not continuous throughout the area of distribution of this type of aboriginal leather armor, its use was not limited to any one subarea.

The aboriginal leather armor just described had a continuous geographic distribution[40] from the Mackenzie basin through the whole Northwest Coast culture area as far south as its southern border near the Hupa in northwestern California, and through the Plateau and Basin[41] areas into the Southwest.[42] In its extreme southern extension in the Southwest it apparently overlapped the extreme northern extension of the quilted cotton armor tradition of Meso-America. If we may believe Cushing the two traditions actually coexisted among the Pueblo peoples, for "Among the Pueblo tribes, 'they also wore cuirasses of elk or bison skin, or of padded cotton and yucca. . .'"[43] There is also

[34] Worcester, 1944, p. 232.
[35] Hough, 1895, p. 641.
[36] See for example, Lewis and Clark, 1904–05, vol. 3, p. 21; Hough, 1895, p. 646; Hill, W. W., 1936, p. 9.
[37] Lewis and Clark, 1904–05, vol. 3, p. 21.
[38] Morice, 1889–90, p. 140.
[39] Fletcher and La Flesche, 1905–1906, p. 79.
[40] Hough, 1895, p. 632.
[41] Its occurrence among the Paviotso is recorded by Lowie, 1924, p. 245.
[42] Hill, W. W., 1936, p. 9.   [43] Hough, 1895, p. 647.

the report of Melchior Diaz who was sent on a reconnaissance of the Pueblo area just prior to the Coronado expedition in 1540. He was unable to reach the Pueblo region, but drew up a report based on the accounts of a number of Indians who had spent considerable periods of time there. His description of Pueblo architecture is very accurate. His report also states that when the Pueblo Indians "... go to war, they carry shields and wear leather jackets, which are made of cow's hide, colored, and that they fight with arrows and with a sort of stone maul..."[44] However, the records of the Coronado expedition do not mention the use of leather armor by the Pueblo Indians in any of their battles, so it may be that Diaz' Indian informants were actually referring to the Apache when they spoke of leather armor. Some exchange between the northern native leather armor tradition and the Meso-American quilted armor tradition undoubtedly took place here in the Southwest, thus accounting for the unique occurrence of the use of quilting as well as gluing in the manufacture of the Navaho type of leather armor, which was otherwise completely northern in type.[45] There is also positive evidence that the quilting technique was used in the manufacture of at least some of the leather armor of the Northwestern Plains Shoshone and of their Blackfoot opponents. Thus, in 1772, Matthew Cocking's Cree companions showed him "... a Coat without sleeves six fold leather *quilted*,[46] used by the Snake tribe to defend them against the arrows of their adversaries."[47] Later, among the Blackfoot, he noted that "They are all well mounted on light, Sprightly animals; Their Weapons, Bows & Arrows: Several have on Jackets of Moose leather six fold, *quilted*, & without sleeves."[48] These quotations may possibly indicate a further spread of an aspect of the southern quilted armor tradition as an alternate manufacturing method to that of the old native leather armor tradition of the north. The method would then have been carried to the north as an alternative element in the armor complex which was, in turn, a part of the Post-horse—Pre-grun military technique pattern.

Since the Apache already had the native leather armor tradition, what occurred when they came in contact with the leather armor of the Spaniards and adopted the horse and mounted warfare was not a complete copying of the model, but a modification of their own tradition. The technique of manufacture remained as it was, though perhaps supplemented by the alternative use of quilting, but the form of the armor changed in imitation of the Spanish type. That is, it now had two arm holes and was no longer open along the right side. Furthermore, it was

[44] Winship, 1892–1893, p. 548.
[45] Hill, W. W., 1936, p. 9.
[46] Italics FRS.
[47] Burpee, 1909, p. 110.
[48] *Ibid.*, p. 111. Italics FRS.

thicker, longer, and slit in the midline, front and back, so that the wearer could straddle his mount. Also, leather armor was provided, at least for the chest of the horse. The painting of the armor reported by Diaz[49] continued.[50] This new syncretistic leather armor tradition was an integral part of the Post-horse—Pre-gun military technique complex and spread with it widely throughout the Plains.

Leather Armor and Archery Fire

The extreme effectiveness of the leather armor against archery is demonstrated in numerous accounts of battles, especially during the Pueblo Revolt and Reconquest, in which very few Spanish soldiers were killed in open battle, although minor wounds on the extremities were fairly frequent. In contrast, many Indians were killed outright in the battles. For example, in 1694, when part of the Spanish army was in Ute country during De Varga's reconquest of New Mexico,

> In the early morning hours of July 12, while the Spaniards were breaking camp, they were attacked by a large band of Utes, armed with bows and arrows and war clubs. Taken completely off guard, six were wounded before they could gather their wits. The situation was soon under control, however, and when eight Utes had been killed the others fled across the river.[51]

Another example comes from a battle with the Pueblo Indians: "An arrow struck the friar squarely on the lower leg; but he came out unscathed thanks to the protection of his heavy leather boots."[52] Finally, we learn that, in this same period of Reconquest,

> During the two months just passed only one Spanish soldier had lost his life in battle. On the other hand ninety-three rebel Indians had been killed, including those executed . . .[53]

The first recorded instance of the use of this leather armor by Indians is at the time of the Pueblo Revolt in 1680. During the periods of Independence and Reconquest it is frequently mentioned by the Spanish sources, and was apparently as widely used as resources would permit. The entire outfit of the Spanish cavalryman was imitated as far as possible. Some Pueblo warriors even used arquebuses, but their effectiveness was severely limited by the shortage of ammunition. An illustration of the complete adoption of Spanish techniques is seen in the report that, at the siege of Santa Fe in 1694,

---

[49] Winship, 1892–1893, p. 458.
[50] Dunn, W. E., 1910–1911, p. 222. ". . . the Apaches . . . used skin armor, painted variously blue, red, green, or white."
[51] Espinosa, 1942, p. 197.
[52] *Ibid.*, p. 267.
[53] *Ibid.*, p. 272.

... the governor of Pecos, Juan de Ye, [had] come to Varga's tent with reports of secret meetings on the mesa of San Juan between Tewas, Tanos, Picuries, and many Apaches ... The warriors were equipped for war in Spanish fashion, even to leather jackets, leather horse armor, and shields.[54]

Again, later during this same siege, we hear that

About five o'clock a large band of Indians, some three hundred in all, was seen emerging from the dense forests to the north, and making its way down the main road from Tesuque. Warriors on foot led the way followed by a cavalry contingent, most of them clothed in leather jackets.[55]

Also, after the siege of Santa Fe, when the conquering army was approaching the Moqui (i. e., Hopi) Pueblos,

Forthwith the Spaniards found themselves in the midst of seven or eight hundred Indians, on horses that were stout and fresh .... Of the eight hundred Indians, over three hundred were heavily armed with lances, bows and arrows, some arquebuses, pistols, and swords.[56]

The fact that the Pueblo Indians, using mainly archery, had many of their warriors killed in battle with the Spaniards, even though numbers of them wore leather armor, while the reverse was the case with the similarly protected Spaniards who used the arquebus, is proof of the vital importance of the gun to Spanish dominion in this area. The arquebus had little more range than the bow, but its much greater penetrating power rendered armor relatively useless against it.[57] Thus,

[54] *Ibid.*, p. 151.   [55] *Ibid.*, p. 68.   [56] *Ibid.*, p. 95.
[57] As a confirmation of this point it is interesting to note a comparison of the effectiveness of the long bow and hand firearms in the 1580's by an English professional soldier. This was still in the period of transition from the bow to the gun as the main reliance for fire-power. Thus, he says, "And nowe for that the Arquebuze, was the first weapon that I did use, I will therefore say something touching the same: it is a weapon most offencive, that as yet ever was invented, for all manner of service, as well on horsebacke as on foote, and in the hands of a skilfull souldier, well practiced and trained with the use thereof, a most terrible and deadly weapon ...." (Barwick, 1580–90, p. 8). "Againe, did not the Duke of Bedford arme the most parte of his Souldiours with tanned leather for the cheefe partes of their bodies, at such time as he was commaunded by that prudent Prince Henry the 7. the 2. yeere of his raigne, to encounter with that Rebell the L. Louell: whereas now by reason of the force of weapons, neither horse nor man is able to beare armours sufficient to defend their bodies from death, whereas in the former times afore mentioned, wounds was the worst to have been doubted, touching the force of all their Archers, as by that manner of arming it seemeth most certaine ...." (*Ibid.*, Introduction). "... whereas Manuell the Emperor of Constantinople, had in his armour or Target the number of 30 arrows sticking: one Harquebuze or Musket shot would have dispatched the matter...." (*Ibid.*, p. 2). "The muskets are weapons of great force ... for few or no armours, will or can defend the force thereof, being neerehand, which is as well a terror to the best armed, as to the meanest: ...." (*Ibid.*, p. 11).
Regarding the effectiveness of the rapid rate of fire of the bow relative to the penetrative power of the gun, our source relates the following discussion: "For

2*

the use of leather armor by the Indians did not help them against the Spaniards, but its use by the Spaniards was almost complete protection against the Indians' archery fire. Luckily for the Spaniards, the gun could be made a nearly perfect monopoly, because of the complexity of the processes involved in its manufacture. The same applied to its ammunition, a constant supply of which was necessary for the gun to be of any value.

It is noteworthy that some articles in this armament complex were more easily acquired than others. Thus, the Indians could manufacture their own leather armor. They could steal horses and small metal cutting tools, since the former were scattered on the range and, though large, could be moved off under their own power, while the latter were small enough and plentiful enough to make theft fairly easy. The gun, however, was a relatively large object and fairly scarce, and hence effectively guarded. It had to be fought for. Furthermore, the existence of a relatively strong, centralized political-military organization made the control of distribution of ammunition in the frontier areas quite effective.

Apache as Carriers of Post-Horse—Pre-Gun Pattern

The first unmistakable record of mounted Indians using the leather armor dates from the year of the Pueblo Revolt in 1680. However, references to its use by the Apache in Texas in 1691,[58] and by the Caddoans in east Texas and Oklahoma in 1690,[59] suggest that diffusion of this trait began earlier than 1680. It is probable that this diffusion was con-

in troth when I was in the French Kings service amongst the olde bandes of footmen, I did greatly commende the force of the Long-bowe, but how was I answered; to be shorte even thus, ... No, no, English man faith be, your case is become fowle, for God hath given us means to encounter with you after another sorte than in times past, for nowe faith be the weakest of us are able to give greater wounds, then the greatest and strongest archer you have: When I replyed, as sir John Smith often dooth that the number of arrows dooth come so thicke, that it was lyke unto haile: well saith he but it is not to be feared, as that weapon that dooth kill where it lights: for faith be, when I doo marche directlye upon them and seeing them coming, I doo stoupe a little with my head, to that ende my Burgonet shall save my face, and seeing the same arrows lighting upon my heade peece or upon my brest, ..., and so seeing the same, to be of no more force nor hurtfull: then doo I with less feare then before, boldelye advance forwards to encounter with them." (*Ibid.*, p. 15).

[58] Dunn W. E., 1910–1911, p. 203.

[59] French, 1851, p. 77. "We reached Cadadoquis on the 10th of May ... I forgot to say that the savages who have horses use them both for war and for hunting. They make pointed saddles, wooden stirrups, and *body-coverings of several skins, one over the other, as a protection from arrows. They arm the breast of their horses with the same material*, a proof that they are not very far from the Spaniards." Italics FRS.

nected with the Apache expansion from about 1650 onwards. The alternative hypothesis, which seems most improbable, is that the complex of the mounted warrior armed with bow, metal-tipped lance, and with leather armor for both horse and rider first spread to the Pueblo Indians in the year 1680 by means of captured Spanish equipment, and was then transmitted to the Apache of New Mexico, their alternate allies and enemies, who, in turn, transmitted it to the Apache of Texas, who again passed it on to the Caddoans of east Texas and Oklahoma, all within the short space of a decade. The sheer physical distance is very great, as is, relative to the time, the number of quite different cultures involved in this chain of diffusion: that is, Spanish, Puebloan, Apache, and Caddoan.

Although the Apache were always fairly active in raiding and war in the New Mexico area, there appears to have been a steady increase in these activities beginning somewhere around 1630 and leveling off near 1660. At the latter date Apache raiding and warfare had attained a high intensity which was maintained until the Pueblo Revolt of 1680. According to Haines,[60] the Indians in the New Mexico area began adopting the horse around 1630. There is evidence that the intensified Apache raiding which began about this time was directed mainly toward acquiring horses. It therefore seems reasonable to suppose that this increased need for horses was engendered by the Apache expansion. For instance, in 1638 we hear the following from Father Juan de Prada:

> These encomenderos are under obligations to participate with their arms and horses in the defense both of the natives as well as of the religious who are in the frontier pueblos and live in constant danger from the Apache Indians. These are a very warlike people, who live in rancherias in the environs of the converted pueblos, against which that nation [Apache] makes continuous attacks.[61]

While in 1661, we hear from Captain Hurtado that

> In these pueblos they [i. e., Apache] have killed some Christian Indians and have carried off others alive to perish in cruel martyrdom. They have also driven off some herds of horses and mares.[62]

Finally, the following statement from Fray Juan Bernal in 1669 gives a picture of the period following 1660:

> ... the whole land is at war with the widespread heathen nation of the Apache Indians, who kill all the Christian Indians they can find and encounter. No road is safe; everyone travels at risk of his life for the heathen traverse them all, being courageous and brave, and they hurl themselves at danger like people who know no God nor that there is any hell.[63]

[60] Haines, F., 1938b, p. 429. See also Worcester, 1944, p. 226.
[61] Bandelier and Hackett, vol. 3, 1937, p. 110.
[62] Ibid., p. 187.
[63] Ibid., p. 272.

In order to give the process of Apache expansion to southeast and northeast a sufficient time span, we must assume that it began at least around 1650–1660, for by the early 1680's the Indians of southwest and west Texas were pleading for Spanish help against the Apache attack. For instance, from the "Itinerary of Juan Dominguez de Mendoza" in 1684 we read that

> Maestre de Campo Juan Dominguez de Mendoza, commander and chief of this detachment of soldiers which is going to the discovery of the East and the kingdom of the Texas at the petition of Don Juan Sabeata, an Indian of the Jumana nation, who, with the other chiefs of that nation went to petition before the Señor Captain Don Domingo Jironsa Petris de Cruzate, governor and captain-general of these provinces of New Mexico ... in order that they might be protected from both directions, by both spiritual and temporal care ... on the 17th day of the said month and year ... arrived at this place where we found a populous rancheria, besides others which we passed, all of the Suma nation, poor people who live chiefly on mescal, which is baked palms. *All these rancherias asked of me aid and help against the common enemy, the Hapaches nation,* alleging generally that most of them were already disposed to becoming Christians. In fact a considerable portion of them were already reducing themselves to settlements and *alleging that the Apaches did not allow them in their* lands.[64]

Likewise, in 1688 Don Pedro Romeros Posada tells that the tribes in the region of the Nueces River have been evicted because of the Apache war.[65] Further east in east Texas, "Hidalgo tells us that, in August 1692, the soldiers joined the Texas in a campaign against the Apaches, going westward until the land of the enemy was reached."[66] Also, we find that the tribes east of the middle Colorado River of Texas had an alliance against the Apache dating prior to the Spanish foundation of San Antonio. When Tonty, in 1690, found the Caddoans at Cadodoquis using leather armor for horse and rider, he took it as proof of contact with the Spaniards,[67] but this appears to have been a mistake, since the only Spanish post anywhere in this area was established in the very year of his own trip. The most likely explanation is that this trait was a result of fairly prolonged hostile contact with the Apache.

Effects of Post-Horse — Pre-Gun Pattern on Trade and Political Organization

In the early phase of Apache expansion the impact of armored horsemen upon unarmored footmen was apparently nearly as devastatingly effective as the Spanish cavalry of Coronado and De Soto had been. Thus, the Apache were able to expand eastward into central Texas, central and western Oklahoma, Kansas, and western Nebraska,

[64] Bolton, 1916, p. 320. Italics FRS.
[65] Paredes, 1686, p. 220.
[66] Dunn, W. E., 1910–1911, p. 204.
[67] French, 1851, p. 77.

as well as to occupy all of eastern New Mexico and Colorado. In the process of displacing their enemies from desirable lands the Apache discovered an additional motive for war. This was the taking of captives for sale to the Spaniards. They were well aware of the great desire of the Spaniards of New Mexico for slaves, having themselves long been a source of supply. Concerning this latter point our records are clear. One states that

> .... Very great, Sir, has been the covetousness of the governors of this king-dom, wherein they have, under color of chastizing the neighboring enemy [i. e., the Apache], made opportunity to send, apparently in the service of his majesty, squadrons of men to capture the heathen Indians [i. e., the Apache] to send them to the camp and mines of El Parral to sell (as governor Don Bernardo Lopez de Mendizabal is doing at present, he having sent there more than seventy Indian men and women to be sold). This is a thing which his Majesty and the señores viceroys have forbidden, under penalty of disgrace, deprivation of office, and loss of property, but no attention is paid to the order, on account of the great interests involved .... For this purpose of making captives, the governor on the fourth of September in this year 1659, sent out an army of eight hundred Christian In-dians and forty Spaniards...[68]

Another Spaniard tells us the monetary value of an Indian slave, stating that "...for the sum of twenty-six pesos one could buy an Apache women as a bond servant."[69]

By taking captives in the course of their wars instead of killing all of the enemy it was possible for the Plains Apache to add another "cash crop" to their resources for trade with the Spaniards. Their new economy created a continuing strong need for replenishing the supply of horses and European metal goods.

There were two ways to satisfy this need, and the Apache employed both. One was to raid the source of supply in New Mexico and carry off the desired goods. This method was very commonly used during the 60's and 70's of the 17th century, and was practiced, to some extent, by certain Apache groups in the early 18th century after the return of the Spaniards. In 1669, Fray Bernal tells us that "... the whole land is at war with the widespread heathen nation of the Apache Indians..."[70] while Captain Hurtado states that "They [i. e., the Apache] have also driven off some herds of horses and mules."[71] Fray de Ayeta in 1679 gives a vivid picture of the serious situation caused by the Apache raids, saying that

> It is public knowledge that from the year 1672 until your Excellency adopted measures for aiding that kingdom six Pueblos were depopulated ....[72]

[68] Bandelier and Hackett, vol. 3, 1937, pp. 186–87.
[69] Ibid., p. 244.
[70] Ibid., p. 272.
[71] Ibid., p. 187.
[72] Ibid., p. 298.

However, raiding was hard work and proved so dangerous within the sphere of action of the Spanish cavalry that it was always necessary and desirable to supplement it with the alternative method of trade. The standard commodities offered by the Apache were buffalo hides and meat, horses and captives. These were bartered for maize, cloth, horses, and metal goods. The exchange of buffalo hides and meat for maize and cloth had existed in well developed form prior to the horse-using phase of Apache life, but horses, captives, and metal wares were additional objects for barter characteristic of this later phase.

It appears that in the 17th century horses were so scarce and the demand for them was so great that they were not as often offered by the Apache in trade as they were in the later 18th and early 19th centuries. Yet, at all times they were the easiest item to steal because they did not need to be carried. And since they were highly valued by both Spaniard and Indian, they were in the nature of a medium of exchange. Thus it was that the Apaches found it profitable to steal Spanish horses and then trade them back to the Spaniards and Pueblo Indians for maize, cloth, and metal goods which were more difficult to carry off.

The Apache wars to the east depended on this trade and therefore stimulated it further. For one thing, the Apache warriors needed the metal goods as part of their equipment. They needed saber blades to tip their lances, and found knives most useful in close combat. They also desired metal bits and stirrups and steel for arrowheads. However, it is probable that the warrior's need for horses was most important and was often satisfied by trading. Trading was further stimulated when the Apache acquired captives from their wars, thereby adding an item which was greatly desired by the Spaniards.[73]

The conditions of Post-horse—Pre-gun warfare appear to have led the Apache to the development of centralized controls over some of the activities of relatively large numbers of people. While it is true that the elaborate equipment of the armored cavalryman gave him a great advantage over the unarmored foot soldiers, still the large numbers of warriors that could be assembled by the populous Caddoan horticulturalists made at least a fair-sized cavalry force necessary for sure victory. Moreover, the horse made it possible to assemble a number of local groups to form one large functional group during a certain portion of the nomadic-hunting phase of the annual economic cycle. The existence of these assemblies was based upon and limited by the habits of the bison, which congregated in huge massed herds during the breeding season, from July through September, and in the coldest months of the winter. When the bison were in these great herds, large regions between the herds were totally devoid of these animals. Thus,

[73] Thomas, 1935, p. 13; Bandelier and Hackett, 1937, vol. 3, pp. 191, 216, 401; Scholes, 1935, p. 109; Paredes, 1686, p. 219.

given a potential for rapid, extensive mobility by the horse, any population that was living by hunting at such a period would be forced to
gather into a large group near the large herd which was the source of
game. At such a period, with the population concentrated in a big camp,
the problem of mustering a large expeditionary force was easily solved.
However, at all other periods of the year, with the exception of short
migration phases in spring and fall, the bison were scattered rather
uniformly over the land in a great number of very small herds, and
this condition forced the population to break apart into small bands in
order to secure sufficient game.[74] Also, during the horticultural phase of
the economic cycle, when the population was scattered about in the
various rancherias, it was a real problem to assemble the necessary
number of warriors for an expedition. This need was apparently answered by developing the institution of one supreme war chief to whom
the war chiefs of a number of bands were subordinated even when the
bands were separated. Upon receiving orders from the head war chief the
subordinate war chiefs would appear, each heading a contingent of the
requested size, at a prearranged place from which the expedition would
set out. Loot was divided and apportioned by the supreme war chief.
Moreover, no expeditions could set forth without his consent. As an
illustration of this organization it is recorded that in Texas at one time
in the early 18th century, when the Spaniards were attempting to arrange
a peace with the Apache,

> The Indians with whom they treated said that they were divided into five tribes
> ("naciones"), each of which was governed by its own chief or capitán. All of these
> chiefs, however, recognized the authority of a head chief (capitán grande), who
> lived still farther north. The squaw sent as a messenger by Flores described the
> method of the Apaches in making a raid, ... She said that all of the five chiefs
> would assemble and furnish about twelve men each for the raid. When these
> returned, the booty was divided and all returned to their respective homes.
> Without the permission of the capitán grande, however, she said, none of the
> chiefs dared to make an expedition.[75]

In addition, at the same general period, but far to the north in central
Kansas, the same type of organization for war is indicated in one of the
speeches made to Bourgmont by the Grand Chief of the Paduca (i. e.,
Apache), in the main village:

> My father, you see there a great number of warriors, but you only see a quarter
> of all those under my domination ... you see there twelve villages which are
> obedient to me... and I say to you and promise that if you have need of 2,000
> warriors, you have only to speak ... they will all follow me for your service ....[76]

The tactics employed by the Apache cavalry were suited to the individual circumstances of the battle, but they utilized ambush, surprise

[74] See Hornaday, 1887, pt. 2, pp. 396, 415–16, 420; Soper, 1941, pp. 391–92.
[75] Dunn, W. E., 1910–1911, p. 221.
[76] Margry, 1879–1888, vol. 6, pp. 440–441.

and mobility to the full. This was due not only to the potentialities of mounted warfare, but also to the need to conserve manpower because of the relatively small Apache population. If the opposing force was small in size and the Apache force large, a favorite battle formation was to advance in a crescent-shaped line with the ends thrown forward to outflank and surround the enemy as rapidly as possible. An example of this formation may be seen in an action which took place in Texas in the early 18th century between a small Spanish force and a much larger Apache one. Our source says

> ... the Spaniards did not number more than twenty-five men, in all, while, according to Almazan, just as they arrived about five hundred Indians came out from their hiding places, all on horseback and well armed. The combined force now attacked the soldiers with great fierceness, forming their line of battle in the shape of a great crescent (media luna), and gradually surrounding the small band[77].

These tactics of surprise and encirclement may well have been developed in the mounted bison hunt and then transferred to the field of battle. Where their opponents were too numerous to be surrounded, the Apache adopted a straight line formation and carried on the battle with fire by the bow and shock with the lance and war club. A battle which took place in northern Texas in the early 18th century illustrates this alternative pattern. In this engagement, although the Apache outnumbered the Spaniards (700 Apache against 100 Spaniards), they did not have a large enough margin to carry out a surrounding or double outflanking movement. Each side drew up a straight line of cavalry opposing the enemy. The source relates that

> The Indians were well disciplined, and showed extraordinary courage. They were on horseback, and were armed with leather breastplates, which no lance or arrow could penetrate. They waited until the soldiers had discharged their guns, and then closed in with them in a hand-to-hand struggle. These tactics were used repeatedly throughout the battle. .... The battle continued for about five hours, but the advantage of the Spaniards' firearms could not be overcome by the Indians, and at about one o'clock they retired, having been entirely driven out of their rancherias. Bustillo estimated the number of Indians killed at two hundred.[78]

Interestingly enough, neither the Apache nor any of the other Indian groups beyond them that took over the Post-horse—Pre-gun military technique complex ever adopted the use of the sword, which has been an inseparable part of the European cavalry complex until practically the present day. For some reason, the mounted Indians retained the use of the war club for close combat, although the Apache, at least, would have had no difficulty in obtaining swords from the Spaniards, since they regularly traded for saber blades, which they then proceeded to convert

---

[77] Dunn, W. E., 1910–1911, p. 226.
[78] *Ibid.*, p. 231.

into lance heads. The failure of the Apache to adopt the sword helped to maintain their habit of mounting the horse from the right side. Apparently, it is most natural for a right-handed man to mount a horse from the right.[79] However, the European cavalryman had to wear the long sword on his left side, so that it might be easily drawn by his right arm, and this, in turn, forced the soldier to mount from the left side. Since the Indian did not take over the sword, his left side was free, and he adopted the more natural habit for a right-handed person of mounting from the right.

It is apparent that the Plains peoples were rather pragmatic in their adoption of the Spanish cavalry complex. This conclusion does not seem to confirm Wissler's[80] opinion that the riding complex of the Spaniards was copied in a slavish fashion without regard to function. His contention was based chiefly on the fact that Indian saddles were completely covered by hides in imitation of the completely covered Spanish saddles, although it would have been sufficient to secure the joints of the wooden frame with bindings. This argument seems inadequate, since Wissler ignores the obvious function of a complete leather covering in providing a more comfortable surface than a hard wooden frame.

Diffusion beyond the Apache

The great success of the Apache armored cavalry forced neighboring groups to adopt this complex themselves as rapidly as possible in order to survive. According to Tonty, by 1690 the Caddoans of eastern Oklahoma had taken over many items. They had begun to use horses for war and for hunting, and they were equipped with the Spanish type of pointed[81] saddle, with stirrups, and with multiple-layered leather armor for horse and rider. However, the complex was not as fully elaborated as it was among the Apaches; for example, they substituted wooden for metal stirrups. They were also very short of horses.

In 1719, La Harpe reports the Caddoans along the Arkansas River in eastern Oklahoma as using leather armor, bridles, and high-pommeled, high-cantled saddles.[82] Apparently horses, although still fairly scarce,

[79] As an example we may cite the highly interesting parallel of the equestrian Abipone of Paraguay in the mid–18th century. They, too, were a people who adopted the horse from the Spaniards. They fought with lance and bow, but without the sword. "The men leap onto their horse on the right side. With the right hand they grasp the bridle, with the left a very long spear, leaning upon which they jump up with the impulse of both feet, and then fall right upon the horse's back." (Dobrizhoffer, 1822, p. 113).

[80] Wissler, 1915b.

[81] The word "pointed" here refers to the fact that the saddle was the high-pommeled, high-cantled type.

[82] Lewis, Anna, 1924, p. 346.

were relatively more plentiful than they had been among the Caddoans
of this general area in 1690. Moreover, some of the chiefs now had
especially fine horses equipped with Spanish-type saddles and bridles.
These people were practicing an annual subsistence cycle like that of
the Apache; they engaged in horticulture in permanent villages in the
spring and summer, supporting themselves mainly on the maize stored
from their previous year's harvest, and they hunted the bison in nomadic
camps in fall and winter.[83]

Likewise, in 1719, at the time of Du Tisne's visit, the Pawnee of the
Kansas area had a barely sufficient supply of horses, which they used
in fighting. The warriors were equipped with leather armor and were
armed with a bow and a lance tipped by a sword blade.[84] Furthermore,
he states that they were violent enemies of the Paduca (i. e., Apache)
to the west, who Bourgmont, in 1724, found using this same war equipment.[85]

In the areas to the north and northwest of the Apache a similar
diffusion of the Post-horse—Pre-gun military technique complex was in
process. The Ute and the Comanche tribes, being the Apache's nearest
neighbors in these directions, were the first to be affected. The Ute had
been on quite friendly terms with the Spaniards during the whole
period up to the Pueblo Revolt of 1680. The first instance of their use
of horses is reported during De Varga's campaign in 1692, when he
found them as mounted allies of the Moqui (i. e., Hopi).[86] It is possible
that some Utes may have been using leather armor and lances, for it is
evident that some Hopi were so equipped. However, in 1694 De Varga's
army was attacked by mistake by a band of Utes who were apparently
on foot.[87] This would lead us to believe that the transition to mounted
warfare was under way, but still incomplete, in the last part of the
17th century.

Several other facts suggest that the Ute's integration of this military
technique pattern was incomplete at this time. For one thing, their
peaceful relations with the Spaniards during this period constitute
evidence that the tribe had no motivation to steal horses. In contrast
with the Apache, the Ute maintained a peaceful trade relation with the
Spaniards all through the 17th century. Indeed, at the end of the
Reconquest of the Pueblos, the Ute were invited to return to trade at
Santa Fe, as had been their custom before 1680.[88]

It is probable that the Ute had either not adopted the horse at all

[83] *Ibid.*, pp. 342, 346.
[84] Margry, 1879–1888, vol. 6, p. 312.
[85] *Ibid.*, p. 445.
[86] Espinosa, 1942, p. 100.
[87] *Ibid.*, p. 197.
[88] *Ibid.*

prior to 1680, or had done so only to a very limited extent. They were a poor people living in a poor land, as Escalante notes, for "... in the plains of the Yutas there are not many buffalo..."[89] Thus, if they had already adopted the complex of cavalry warfare or the mounted nomadic hunting life at this time they could never have acquired enough goods for trade with the Spaniards to satisfy, by that means alone, the great need for horses which would have existed.

However, in the first two decades of the 18th century there occurred a complete reversal in the Ute-Spanish relationship. Horse-thieving by the Utes suddenly became common. The first complaints in this regard were registered around 1704,[90] and by 1719 the raiding had become extremely prevalent. The situation was described by Juan de Archibeque, a member of a council convened at Santa Fe in 1719 to discuss the problem and decide whether or not to go to war. It was his opinion that

> ... war [should] be made against the Ute and Comanche because it is evident that for more than seven or eight years they have come to steal horses and rob herds and run away with the goods in the trade which this kingdom has with the Apaches of El Cuartelejo. Since they have committed three murders, the present is very opportune to make war upon them....[91]

By this later date there is no doubt that the Ute, together with their newly-arrived allies, the Comanche, had adopted both cavalry warfare and the mounted nomadic hunting life with enthusiasm. However, the increasing incidence of horse raiding probably reflects not only the expanding needs of the Ute and Comanche, but also of the eastern Shoshonean groups to the north of them who apparently began to use the horse at this time.

Disassociation of Horticulture and the Horse

Though the Ute and Comanche adopted the horse, they did not take up the combined horticultural and nomadic, bison-hunting annual subsistence cycle that the Apache used. Instead, they became exclusively bison-hunting, nomad horsemen. The reason may be that these people were recent immigrants from a land relatively unfavorable to horticulture. The Comanche, in addition, had lived far from any people who practiced this art. However, the fact that the same conditions which had led the Apache of the Plains to become part-time horticulturalists were working upon the Comanche, although usually entirely counteracted by other factors, is evident in their one voluntary attempt to establish a permanent settlement as a base for summer horticultural activities.

[89] Salmeron, 1626, pp. 90–91.
[90] Thomas, 1935, p. 26.
[91] Ibid., p. 107.

The story is the following: In 1776, a new administrative organization called the "Provincias Internas," was set up in the northern provinces of New Spain. This formed a separate administrative unit under a Commandante-General whose chief task was to control the aggressions of the nomads. Soon thereafter, in 1779, Anza led an expedition against the Comanche in east central Colorado. He met and completely defeated two separate hostile forces, besides killing the Comanche leader, Cuerno Verde. Largely as a result of the increased military effectiveness of the Spaniards, the Comanche and the Ute made peace with them and with each other at Santa Fe in 1786. Then, in 1787, the Jupe group of the Comanche, under their head chief, Paruanarimuco, asked the assistance of the Governor of New Mexico in establishing a pueblo on the Arkansas River in Colorado. This assistance was granted. Several months later, in a letter to the governor's successor, the Commandante-General was able to write that

> The predecessor of your Grace D[n]. Juan Baptista de Anza... indicated to me in an official report of the twentieth of October last the state of the new settlement of San Carlos, established on the Rio Napestle by Lieutenant-General Paruanari-muco. He says, that for this purpose he supplied him with thirty workers, implements and everything else necessary, under the direction of a skilled artisan. There were already at that date, nineteen houses furnished and a large number begun: to this advice his Grace added in a report of the tenth of November, No. 19, that from the sixteenth of September the Comanches were living in them.[92]

However, the conditioning factors of Comanche culture soon returned to their normal balance and the Jupe abandoned San Carlos and horticulture for good in the following January.

Southward Expansion of Pure Nomad Hunters

By approximately the first quarter or the first third of the 18th century, the Ute and Comanche had swept the Apache from the most northern part of their territory and occupied this rich land themselves. The early stages of this great victory of the Comanche over the Apache can be ascribed to two factors. The first is that the Comanche apparently adopted the Apache cavalry equipment. Even as late as the mid-18th century, a battle between the Osage and an allied force of Wichita and Comanche is reported in which the Comanche are clearly possessed of the Post-horse—Pre-gun military technique pattern. The source states that

> ... both together came to a village of the Grands Ossages at a time when a portion of their people were at the Cerne (Surround) killing animals; they fell upon them and so sharp was the attack that the Grands Ossages lost 22 of their chiefs, while the others left 27 of their people on the field of battle .... The

[92] Thomas, 1929, p. 9.

Grands Ossages were surprised at seeing the Laytannes.[93] They dread them greatly
.... *The Laytannes are armed with spears like the ancient Spaniards; they are*
always mounted on caparisoned horses ....[94]

The second factor is that the sedentary spring and summer phase of
Apache life proved to be a great military liability when they were pitted
against a foe always on the move. The Comanche quickly learned the
location of the Apache horticultural rancherias and, at the appropriate
seasons, could be almost certain of finding their foe there. With the
element of uncertainty as to the location of the enemy ruled out, the
Comanche could make telling use of the element of surprise, and thereby
render the Apache war equipment and organization ineffective. This
situation also allowed them to concentrate overwhelming numbers
against the isolated rancherias and eliminate them one by one. As a
Spanish officer reported in 1723,

> ... captains of the heathen Apache nation ... represented to me that the
> heathens of the Comanche nation, their enemies, had attacked them with a large
> number in their rancherias in such a manner that they could not make use of
> weapons for their defense. They launched themselves with such daring and
> resolution that they killed many men, carrying off their women and children as
> captives.[95]

When the Apache attempted to retaliate, after gathering together
contingents from a number of bands, the difficulty of finding and
surprising their erratically moving enemy was very great and caused a
large number of such expeditions to be total failures. The Valverde expedition of 1719, for example, met the assembled Apache forces and
together they wandered about east central Colorado in search of the
Comanche. The only thing they encountered was the rather cold trail
of a large enemy camp which it was then too late in the season to
pursue.[96] Since the Comanche had the effective initiative for nearly half
the year (although circumstances were nearly equalized during the fall
and winter when the Apache became nomads also) the inevitable result
was a series of disasterous defeats for the Apache.

Interestingly enough, there appear to have been two alternative
solutions to the military problem posed by the Comanche, neither of
which the Apache seem to have used. One was for the Apache to abandon
the settled horticultural phase of their annual subsistence cycle and
become complete bison-hunting, mounted nomads like the Comanche.
Indeed, this was the solution adopted by some of the Caddoan tribes of

[93] The Comanche.
[94] Wisconsin Historical Collections, 1908, vol. 18, pp. 87–88. Italics FRS.
[95] Thomas, 1935, p. 194. See also pp. 29, 115; and Bolton, 1915, p. 94.
[96] Thomas, 1935, p. 30.

Oklahoma, the so-called "Wandering Nation,"[97] under the pressure of Apache attacks. The other was to establish compact permanent village sites and fortify them as the Pawnee of Nebraska eventually did,[98] as well as some of the other Caddoans further south. For example, the Taovayas (Wichita) village encountered by Parilla in 1759 on the Red River was completely fortified by a ditch and a stockade.[99] Probably the reason the Apache did not adopt the fortified village solution was that their more arid western country could not have supported any large concentrations of population, since arable sites were small in extent and widely separated.

[97] Regarding the identity of this group, the following quotation refers to the La Harpe expedition in southern Oklahoma along the Red River in 1719:

"The Twenty-ninth, Sieur Du Rivage arrived from his journey with two savages of the Quidehais nation; he reported to me that at seventy leagues on the west side and from the west a fourth northwest he had encountered a party of the *roving nation*, who were the Quidehais, Naouydiches, Joyvan, Huanchane, Huane, Tancoye, ..." (translated from P. Margry in Lewis, Anna, 1924, p. 333. Italics FRS).

The "Wandering Nation" was apparently a functional federation of fragments of Caddoan and non-Caddoan tribes previously broken or displaced by the Apache. They may provisionally be identified as follows:

a) The "Quidehais" were probably the Bidais, a non-Caddoan group. (See Bolton, 1914, vol. 1, p. 20).

b) The "Naoudyches" were probably a part of the Hasinai, a Caddoan group, for "Naouadiche" was the name of the same Hasinai village which La Salle visited in 1687 and Tonty in 1690.

c) The "Huane" were probably the Jumano, a non-Caddoan group. The Jumano tribe originally lived in southwest Texas near the Rio Grande above and below the Pecos River. After adopting the horse they spent the winters in their old homeland and the summers hunting buffalo in central Texas. Apparently under the impact of the Apache expansion a large part of the tribe was permanently driven back to southwest Texas, while the other fragment became a section of the "Wandering Nation." After 1750 there were two groups called Jumano by the Spaniards. One was the original Jumano tribe of southwest Texas while the other was the Taovayas, a Wichita tribe of the Red River of Texas with which the split-off fragment of the original Jumano tribe had apparently amalgamated by this time. (For further discussion of the "Jumano" question see Bolton, 1911, pp. 66–84).

d) The "Tancaoye" were probably the Tonkawa, or a fragment thereof.

[98] Strong, 1935, pp. 57, 298.

[99] Bolton, 1915, p. 89.

CHAPTER THREE

Post-Horse—Pre-Gun Pattern on the Northwestern Plains

Around 1700, various Shoshonean peoples west of the eastern front ranges of the Rocky Mountains appear to have adopted the mounted, nomadic hunting life. They probably obtained the necessary horses from the Utes to the south who raided the primary source of horses in New Mexico. These Shoshoneans then, like the Apache, apparently expanded explosively in all favorable directions. Their movements were, of course, limited by geographic factors. Because of unsuitable climate and vegetation there were few buffalo in the region west of the Rocky Mountains. The east, however, was ideal country for buffalo hunters. Hence, the Shoshoneans probably first advanced directly eastward onto the High Plains through the gap in the Rocky Mountains at South Pass in southwestern Wyoming. From this point on the Plains Shoshonean groups appear to have radiated out to the south, east, and north.

The Comanche traveled south on the High Plains, through excellent buffalo territory, toward the source of horses in New Mexico. The remainder of the Shoshoneans spread out to the east and north over the northern Plains, driving out or exterminating the then inhabitants. The northern neighbors of the Shoshone, the Flathead and Kutenai, soon acquired the horse also, and occupied the most northwesterly Plains. The expansion of these tribes seems to have been well under way by the second decade of the 18th century.

Eventually the Shoshoneans clashed vigorously with the Flathead and Kutenai on the northwest, with the Blackfoot and Atsina on the north, with horticultural village groups, such as the Mandan, Hidatsa and Arikara along the Missouri, on the east, and with the Apache of western Nebraska and northeastern Colorado on the east and south. Some of the northern groups, especially the Blackfoot and the Atsina, were probably experiencing strong pressure in the forest and marginal forest land to the north and east from the gun-equipped Cree and Assiniboin, who at this time were expanding westward in search of new, untapped regions in which to exploit the fur trade.

Earlier History

In the Northwestern Plains area the Pre-horse—Pre-gun military technique pattern apparently took two forms. Both put a premium on numerical strength. The first one, usually preferred, was for a large war party to locate a small, isolated enemy camp, creep up on it during the night, and make a surprise attack at dawn, slaughtering the inhabitants. The second was used when the enemy was too vigilant to allow a successful surprise attack, or when both sides were nearly equal in numbers and confident of victory. Under these conditions the battle was drawn between two opposing lines of infantry, armed with bows, spears, clubs, and very large leather shields, the men separated by about three-foot intervals. The battle began when the lines had advanced to a point within archery range of each other, at which time the warriors, protecting themselves with their shields, sat on the ground and subjected the opposing line to archery fire for a varying period. The next stage of the battle arrived when one side decided to substitute shock for fire. A chief would then lead the whole line in a charge, oftentimes preceded by the singing of a war song, the charge itself being initiated with a war cry. The ensuing hand-to-hand struggle would usually be brief and bloody, and the issue quickly decided. The defeated side would either flee in a complete rout and be hotly pursued by the enemy warriors until the latter halted to struggle among themselves for loot, trophies, and scalps, or, if the defeat were not so severe, they would retreat in a fair state of organization, maintaining the line formation and carrying off their dead and wounded.

Our source for this Pre-horse—Pre-gun phase is the account of Saukamappee given to David Thompson in the winter of 1787–88. Saukamappee was originally a Cree, but as a young man he joined the Piegan tribe of the Blackfoot. In all respects he appears to have been a most reliable informant. At the time of the interviews, Thompson estimated his age between seventy-five and eighty years. His account of the first Snake-Blackfoot battle is as follows:

The Peeagans were always the frontier Tribe, and upon whom the Snake Indians made their attacks, these latter were very numerous, . . . and the Peeagans had to send messengers among us to procure help . . . I was then about his age (pointing to a Lad of about sixteen years) . . . My father brought about twenty [Cree] warriors with him. There were a few guns amongst us, but very little ammunition, and they were left to hunt for the families; Our weapons was a Lance, mostly pointed with iron, some few of stone, A Bow and a quiver of Arrows; the Bows were of Larch, the length came to the chin; the quiver had about fifty arrows, of which ten had iron points, the others were headed with stone. He carried his knife on his breast and his axe in his belt. Such was my fathers weapons, and those with him had much the same weapons. I had a Bow and Arrows and a knife, of which I was very proud. We came to the Peeagans and their allies. They were camped in the Plains on the left bank of the River (the north side) and were a great many. We were feasted, a great War Tent was made, and a few days passed in speeches, feasting and dances. A war chief was elected by the chiefs, and we got ready to march. Our spies had been out and had seen a large camp of the Snake Indians on the Plains of the Eagle Hill, and we had to cross the River in canoes, and on rafts, which we carefully secured for our retreat. When we had crossed and numbered our men, we were about 350 warriors (this he showed by counting every finger to be ten, and holding up both hands three times and then one hand) they had their scouts out, and came to meet us. Both parties made a great show of their numbers, and I thought that they were more numerous than ourselves. After some singing and dancing, they sat down on the ground, and placed their large shields before them, which covered them: We did the same, but our shields were not so many, and some of our shields had to shelter two men. Theirs were all placed touching each other; their Bows were not so long as ours, but of better wood, and the back covered with the sinews of the Bisons which made them very elastic, and their arrows went a long way and whizzed about us as balls do from guns. They were all headed with a sharp, smooth, black stone (flint) which broke when it struck anything. Our iron headed arrows did not go through their shields, but stuck in them; On both sides several were wounded, but none lay on the ground; and night put an end to the battle, without a scalp being taken on either side, and in those days such was the result, unless one party was more numerous than the other. The great mischief of war then, was as now, by attacking and destroying small camps of ten to thirty tents, which are obliged to separate for hunting...[1]

Transition from Shortage to Abundance of Horses

Interestingly enough, during the first phase of their life on the Plains, the Shoshone did not risk their horses in battle, but retained the old Pre-horse—Pre-gun military technique pattern. Apparently, this tribe was so far from the source of horses in New Mexico and had so recently acquired them that they had only the bare minimum required for bison hunting, and could spare none for use in transport or war. Moreover, during this early period the Shoshone were not yet in possession of the full Post-horse—Pre-gun military technique pattern. Specifically, they lacked the leather armor with which the fully equipped tribes to the south protected their horses from the arrows and spears of the enemy, and hence, could not afford to risk their scarce and tremendously valuable horses in war. With regard to the use of the horse for transport by Plains peoples with a very limited supply of horses, Alexander Henry states that among the Assiniboin at the beginning of the 19th century, the "Transportation of their baggage is mostly performed by dogs, as their horses are generally kept for hunting buffalo."[2] We may be sure that horses were more important to the Plains nomads in bison hunting than in either transportation or warfare, since, when tribes had very few horses, they were used entirely in the hunt.

This early phase seems to have continued through 1726–30. Evidently,

[1] Tyrrell, 1916, "Saukamappee's Account," pp. 328–330.
[2] Coues, 1897, p. 517.

some time during this period the first battle between the Snake[3] and the Blackfoot took place as recounted by Saukamappee.[4] By the time the second battle in this account took place, apparently some ten years later (1736–40), the Shoshone were using horses in surprise raids and skirmishes, but still not in large battles. This suggests an increase in the supply of horses, but also indicates that they were still too few to be risked in pitched battle, and further, that the use of leather armor, which would have effectively protected these mounts from the arrows of their enemies, had not yet diffused up from the south.

Saukamappee's description of the second Snake-Blackfoot battle runs as follows:

.... I grew to be a man, became a skilfull and fortunate hunter, and my relations procured me a Wife. She was young and handsome and we were fond of each other. We had passed a winter together, when Messengers came from our allies to claim assistance. By this time the affairs of both parties had much changed; we had more guns and iron headed arrows than before; but our enemies the Snake Indians and their allies had Misstutim (Big Dogs, that is Horses) on which they rode, swift as the Deer, on which they dashed at the Peeagans, and with their stone Pukamoggan knocked them on the head, and they had thus lost several of their best men. This news we did not well comprehend and it alarmed us, for we had no idea of Horses and could not make out what they were. Only three of us went and I should not have gone, had not my wife's relations frequently intimated that her father's medicine bag would be honored by the scalp of a Snake Indian. When we came to our allies, the great War Tent [was made] with speeches, feasting and dances as before; and when the War Chief had viewed us all it was found between us and the Stone Indians we had ten guns and each of us about thirty balls, and powder for the war, and we were considered the strength of the battle. After a few days march our scouts brought us word that the enemy was near in a large war party, but had no Horses with them, for at that time they had very few of them. When we came to meet each other, as usual, each displayed their numbers, weapons and shields, in all which they were superior to us, except our guns which were not shown, but kept in their leathern cases, and if we had shown [them], they would have taken them for long clubs. For a long time they held us in suspense; a tall Chief was forming a strong party to make an attack on our centre, and the others to enter into combat with those opposite to them; We prepared for the battle the best we could. Those of us who had guns stood in the front line, and each of us [had] two balls in his mouth, and a load of powder in his left hand to reload. We noticed they had a great many short stone clubs for close combat, which is a dangerous weapon, and had they made a bold attack on us, we must have been defeated as they were more numerous and better armed than we were, for we could have fired our guns no more than twice; and were at a loss what to do on the wide plain, and each Chief encouraged his men to stand firm. Our eyes were all on the tall Chief and his motions, which appeared to be contrary to the advice of several old Chiefs, all this time we were about the strong flight of an arrow from each other. At length the tall chief retired and they formed their

---

[3] The "Snake" is the name by which the Shoshone are designated in most of the historical documents. Among the modern Shoshone it is the Wind River division which most probably has a direct historic descent from the "Snake" of the early period.

[4] Tyrrell, 1916, pp. 328–330.

long usual line by placing their shields on the ground to touch each other, the shield having a breadth of full three feet or more. We sat down opposite to them and most of us waited for the night to make a hasty retreat. The War Chief was close to us, anxious to see the effect of our guns. The lines were too far asunder for us to make a sure shot, and we requested him to close the line to about sixty yards, which was gradually done, and lying flat on the ground behind the shields, we watched our opportunity when they drew their bows to shoot at us, their bodies were then exposed and each of us, as opportunity offered, fired with deadly aim, and either killed, or severely wounded, every one we aimed at.

The War Chief was highly pleased, and the Snake Indians finding so many killed and wounded kept themselves behind their shields; the War Chief then desired we would spread ourselves by two's throughout the line, which we did, and our shots caused consternation and dismay along their whole line. The battle had begun about Noon, and the Sun was not yet half down, when we perceived some of them had crawled away from their shields, and were taking to flight. The War Chief seeing this went along the line and spoke to every Chief to keep his Men ready for a charge of the whole line of the enemy, of which he would give the signal; this was done by himself stepping in front with his Spear, and calling on them to follow him as he rushed on their line, and in an instant the whole of us followed him, the greater part of the enemy took to flight, but some fought bravely and we lost more than ten killed and many wounded; Part of us pursued, and killed a few, but the chase had soon to be given over, for at the body of every Snake Indian killed, there were five or six of us trying to get his scalp, or part of his clothing, his weapons, or something as a trophy of the battle. As there were only three of us, and seven of our friends, the Stone Indians, we did not interfere, and got nothing.[5]

However, by the time of the expedition of the Chevalier de la Verendrye into the Northern Plains (1742–43), the Shoshone were apparently well supplied with horses and consistently used cavalry in their raids on the villages of their eastern enemies.[6] As a result of the increasing diffusion of horses and other elements of the military technique complex from south to north, the Post-horse—Pre-gun military technique pattern began to take its final shape in the Northwestern Plains, just as it had done in the Southern Plains. The weapons were the lance, bow, war club, and trader's knife. The rider was protected by a small leather shield, easily handled on horseback, and by the recently diffused multi-layered leather cavalry armor. War now consisted of rather infrequent cavalry battles and more regularly skirmishes. The latter usually occurred as unwelcome incidents in the frequent horse-raiding that was conducted by tribes, such as the Blackfoot, who were still relatively ill supplied with horses.[7]

[5] *Ibid.*, pp. 330–332.
[6] Burpee, 1927, p. 411.
[7] For example, Anthony Hendry, in 1754–55, found the Blackfoot thoroughly committed to a mounted, nomadic bison-hunting life. (Burpee, 1907, pp. 307–354. See also Burpee, 1909, pp. 89–121). And still, in 1790, Umfreville remarked that the Blackfoot "... are the most numerous and powerful nation we are acquainted with, ... War is more familiar to them than the other nations, and they are by far the most formidable to the common enemy of the whole [i. e., the Snake]. In

Relation of War and Trade during Northern Shoshonean Advance

This situation probably lasted for about a generation, say from 1735 to 1765, and during this period the Snake had the most horses by virtue of their strategic geographic position of proximity to the source of supply in the south. The pressing need of this tribe for European metal goods, horses, and mules was partially satisfied by direct trade in New Mexico and by trade with Comanche kinsmen to the south who acted as middlemen. The tribe's main problem was to find a commodity of exchange which was sufficiently valuable, transportable, and plentiful to support this trade in some volume. Buffalo hides were not satisfactory, because their relatively low value and large bulk made their transportation for such a tremendous distance hardly worth while. The solution appears to have been a trade in war captives, for such a commodity was not only valuable but, in addition, could transport itself to market. And the need for captives further stimulated the warfare with the surrounding tribes that had originally been started by the physical expansion of the Snake into the Northern Plains. The Snake raided for captives continuously and on a large scale, in order to exchange them for goods and horses in the south, while the victimized tribes raided for vengeance and to acquire badly needed horses, so that they might equip themselves fully for war and the mounted, nomadic hunting life.[8]

A quotation from Matthew Cocking illustrates how wide the radius of action of the Snake was and how greatly they were feared, even in 1772–73. Cocking came up the Saskatchewan River with a band of Cree who annually made a trading trip to Hudson Bay. As soon as they began to enter into the border area of the Plains the Cree became nervous. One journal entry states that "The natives saw a Strange Horse today & suppose it belongs to the Snake Indians, their Enemies."[9] And a few days later he notes that the "Indians killed several Buffalo. The Natives in general [here he refers to the Assiniboin and Blackfoot as well as the Cree] are afraid of the Snake Indians & say they are nigh at hand."[10]

During this period, while the Post-horse—Pre-gun military technique pattern was spreading from southwest to northeast, the Post-gun—Pre-horse military technique pattern was advancing to meet it. We turn now to a description of the latter pattern.

their inroads into the enemies' country, they frequently *bring off a number of horses, which is their principal inducement in going to war.*" (Umfreville, 1790, p. 200. Italics FRS).

[8] Burpee, 1927, pp. 411, 415–16, 426, footnote, p. 427; Margry, 1879–88, vol. 6, pp. 458, 644, 650–51.

[9] Burpee, 1909, p. 106.

[10] *Ibid.*

CHAPTER FOUR

DEVELOPMENT OF POST-GUN–PRE-HORSE PATTERN

Early Synthesis in the Northeastern Forest Area

The Post-gun—Pre-horse military technique pattern had developed in all the forest area to the east and north of the Plains as soon as trade, chiefly the fur trade, had made a regular supply of guns and ammunition available. Several different forms were employed. The particular one used depended on the type of warfare considered most suitable for the particular enemy confronted. In the Cree-Athabascan war, the Athabascans were separated from the fur trading posts by their Cree enemies, and were thus totally without firearms. They were also scattered in very small, isolated camps, particularly in the winter, since they maintained themselves by hunting in a heavily forested environment. Under these circumstances the Cree found it best to divide their force during the winter campaign season into small groups of several families each, which would then disperse to hunt down the helpless enemy with their guns like another form of game. This type of warfare proved highly advantageous to the Cree: they were able to conquer new areas rich in beaver, and also captured furs which were a means of exchange for European goods, particularly for the ever-needed guns and ammunition. Furthermore, the captured women and children were a source of additional numerical strength.[11] In Mackenzie's day, 1789–93, this war was largely over, and the Cree had even withdrawn from the area of the upper Churchill River,

... for since traders have spread themselves over it, it is no more the rendezvous of the errant Knisteneaux [i. e., Cree], part of whom used annually to return thither from the country of the Beaver River, which they had explored to its source in their war and hunting excursions, and as far as the Saskatchiwine, where they sometimes met people of their own nation, who had prosecuted similar conquests up that river.[12]

He goes on to relate that, prior to the spread of the traders when the predatory Cree were still advancing,

The spring was the period of this joyful meeting, when their time was occupied in feasting, dancing, and other pastimes, which were occasionally suspended for sacrifice, and religious solemnity: while the narratives of their travels, and the history of their wars, amused and animated the festival. The time of rejoicing was but short, and was soon interrupted by the necessary preparations for their annual

[11] Tyrrell, 1934, p. 551.
[12] Mackenzie, 1902, vol. I, p. CXXVII.

journey to Churchill, to exchange their furs for such European articles as were now become necessary to them. The shortness of the seasons, and the great length of their way requiring the utmost dispatch, the most active men of the tribe, with their youngest women, and a few of their children undertook the voyage, under the direction of some of their chiefs, following the waters already described, to their discharge at Churchill Factory .... There they remained no longer than was sufficient to barter their commodities, with a supernumerary day or two to gratify themselves with the indulgence of spirituous liquors. At the same time the inconsiderable quantity they could purchase to carry away with them, for a regale with their friends, was held sacred, and reserved to heighten the enjoyment of their return home, when the amusements, festivity, and religious solemnities of the spring were repeated. The usual time appropriated to these convivialities being completed, they separated, to pursue their different objects; and if they were determined to go to war, they made the necessary arrangements for their future operations.[13]

Although, by 1791, the Athabascans had armed themselves to a point where they were almost able to halt the Cree aggression, there were still some few who lacked firearms, and upon these the Cree still preyed. Thus, in that year in the region of Lake Athabaska, Peter Fidler met

... 4 Canoes of Southern Indians[14] of the Beaver river, 7 men & 3 women, who are returning back to their own Country from War, they went in the Spring and the Cree that accompanied us all Summer was their relation & missed them in the Athapescow Lake & prevented his accompanying them .... They had the Scalps of 2 Men .... They also killed one Woman. They met them coming towards the Slave Lake House as they supposed to Trade as they had a few Beaver skins with them, with hatchets, Ice chisels &c marked on them probably these were the articles they wished to purchase.... They were of the Dog ribbed tribe — & use Canoes. They got from those they killed Several arrows shod with a kind of hard stone resembling flint, a Bow or 2 of very clumsy workmanship, a small old Knife & a Bayonet made by themselves from either an Ice chisel or a Hatchet, but both of them very rudely constructed... they appeared very much elated at their success — barberous rascals. As they had no ammunition & Tobacco, I gave them 10 Ball (they having powder of their own)...[15]

Finally, Mackenzie illustrates the dread which the Cree had formerly inspired, and continued to inspire, in tribes without guns. While he was traveling down the Mackenzie River through Athabascan country in 1789, he caught sight of a tall hill, which he climbed out of curiosity. When he reached the top, he

... was very much surprised to find it crowned by an encampment. The Indians informed me, that it is the custom of the people who have no arms to choose these elevated spots for the places of their residence, as they can render them unacces-

---

[13] *Ibid.*, pp. CXVII–CXXIX. For the Cree-Athabascan war, see also Mandelbaum, 1940; Franklin, 1823, pp. 56, 69, 106; Mackenzie, 1902, vol. 1, pp. CXII–CXIII, CXIX, CXXII–CXXIII, CXXXVIII–CXXXIX, 195, 215–16, 230–31, 237, 241–42, 326, 337, 340–41; vol. 2, pp. 14, 22–23, 59, 75–76, 88–89, 92–93, 98, 157.

[14] A name applied to the Cree by the Hudson's Bay people.

[15] Tyrrell, 1934, p. 498.

sible to their enemies, particularly the Knisteneaux [i. e., Cree], of whom they are in continual dread.[16]

Under certain circumstances the Cree abandoned this warfare pattern of small scattered groups of attackers in favor of a pattern using large, concentrated expeditionary forces. The latter tactic was required during their warfare with the Sioux. In the early phases of the war between the Sioux and the Cree-Assiniboin allies, the Sioux, though lacking firearms, were concentrated in fair-sized villages in certain areas, and in others, although more dispersed, were quickly assembled at the threat of war.

Such large expeditionary forces were assembled in the spring or summer at the lakes where it was customary for the Cree to gather for fishing at this season. Thus, one spring while on his fourth voyage, 1661–64, Radisson was in western Wisconsin some distance from the south shore of Lake Superior. Here there assembled a great number of Sioux from the Mille Lacs region to decide whether to make war on the Cree and also to try to make an alliance with the French, believing as Radisson tells us "... that the true means to gett the victory was to have a thunder. They meant a gune, calling it miniskoick."[17]

Trying to make peace between the two, he made a trip at this time over a considerable distance to the Cree on the north shore of Lake Superior where he found "There were above 600 men in a fort, with a great deal of baggage on their shoulders...."[18] The Cree were also holding a council to decide on an expedition against the Sioux.

In order to suggest the large size and unified nature of the forces often employed in warfare in this region, the Ottawa-Huron campaign of 1672 against the Sioux is cited here. The allies

... went down to Montreal, and bought in exchange for their peltries, only guns and munitions of war — intending to march against the Scioux, build a fort in their country, and wage war against them during the entire winter. Returning home after this trading expedition, they hastily gathered in their grain-crops, and all departed in a body to march against the Scioux... [and together with the Potawatomi, the Sauk and the Fox they] formed *a body over a thousand men*, all having guns or other powerful weapons of defense.[19]

The necessity for such a large force becomes apparent in the following quotation:

As soon as they arrived in the Scioux country, they fell upon some little villages, putting the men to flight and carrying away the women and children whom they found there. This blow was so quickly dealt that they had not time to reconnoiter or to erect fortifications. The fugitives quickly carried the alarm to the neighboring

---

[16] Mackenzie, 1902, vol. 1, p. 228.
[17] Radisson, 1885, p. 213.
[18] *Ibid.*, p. 218.
[19] Blair, 1911, p. 188. Italics FRS.

villages, the men of which hastened in crowds to fall upon their enemies, and so vigorously attacked them that they took to flight.[20]

Again, in the late 1670's or early 1680's, "Twelve hundred Nadouais-sioux, Sauteurs, Ayoes, and even some Outaouaks[21] were then on the march against the Outagamis and Maskoutechs[22]..."[23] The pattern of war illustrated above, using the gun and large expeditions, was essentially the same as that of the Northeastern Woodland area and was indeed heavily influenced by eastern tribes such as the Huron and Ottawa, who had fled west to escape the Iroquois.[24]

Spread into the Northwestern Forest Area

As the Cree-Assiniboin war machine expanded, it at first evicted the Sioux from northern Minnesota,[25] but it was shortly blocked from further southern expansion, as the Sioux gradually acquired guns through the French fur trade. Having exploited the beaver resources of this new territory and the old home area to the point of diminishing returns, the allies advanced toward the fresh regions of the west, with the Assiniboin occupying the southernmost part of the front and the Cree the remainder toward the north.[26] Hence, in the late 17th century and the earliest part of the 18th century the allies gradually invaded the Red River and Lake Winnipeg area, and then worked west up the Assiniboin and the lower Saskatchewan Rivers. At this time the native inhabitants of the northeastern prairie land were in the Pre-horse—Pre-gun stage and, like the Cheyenne a bit to the south, were probably living in sedentary horticultural villages and making seasonal hunting expeditions. They were driven from their homeland gradually but inexorably by the large, gun-equipped expeditions of the allies, who then proceeded to exploit the territory with the same techniques that they had used in their native northern forest lands. The displaced natives moved out west and south from the marginal area into the true Plains. The Cree-Assiniboin invaders did not follow them for the sufficient reasons that beaver were much less plentiful there and the environment no longer suitable for exploitation by the techniques of the Northern Forest. Because of this ecological barrier, the Assiniboin and Cree swept on to the west, keeping north of the true Plains, and occupying

---

[20] *Ibid.*, p. 189. It is also obvious that the Sioux must have made good progress in getting firearms by this time, or such a victory would have been impossible.

[21] Sioux, Ojibwa, Iowa, and Ottawa.

[22] Fox and Mascoutin.

[23] Blair, 1911, vol. 2, p. 112.

[24] For further discussion of Post-gun—Pre-horse warfare, see Chapter VI, especially pp. 67–69.

[25] See Hyde, 1937, pp. 6–12.

[26] See Mandelbaum, 1940, pp. 174–187; also Hyde, 1933, pp. 6–14, 20, 39.

the belt transitional between Plains and Northern Forest as far as the barrier of the Rockies.

Ecological Limitation to Spread of the Gun

Interestingly enough, because of the conditions of the fur trade at this period in the Northwest country, the ecological discontinuity also prevented the spread of the Post-gun—Pre-horse military technique pattern onto the Northwestern Plains. Likewise, after the Post-horse— Pre-gun military technique pattern had spread over this whole Plains area, this same situation prevented the two patterns from becoming completely fused and reorganized into the final Horse *and* Gun pattern until the early 19th century. This latter development occurred only after changes in the conditions of the fur trade had taken place.

During the latter part of the 17th century and the first three-quarters of the 18th century the Hudson's Bay Company traded primarily for beaver, and secondarily for the valuable furs of other small northern forest animals. This specialization was due chiefly to the difficulty in transporting large shipments of bulky trade items through the territory. Cargo could be transported to the Bay only by canoe with portages, so that traders found their greatest profit lay in handling numerous, small, light units of high individual value. Although the hides of large animals did have a market in Europe, their value was relatively low in proportion to their weight and bulk. Thus, as long as beaver and similar furs were available in the general trade area they were always selected in place of the large hides. Furthermore, while it is true that the beaver was found in the territory of the true Plains peoples, it was as a part of the Woodland biome[27] which formed small scattered islands within the vast Plains biome. Particularly after the assimilation of the horse, the Plains peoples increasingly adapted their culture to the Plains biome, and it is apparent that, with increasing specialization, the techniques of exploiting these two differing biomes became mutually exclusive in nature. The coat of the beaver was in marketable condition only in the cold half of the year. The trapping season was further limited to the fall and spring months, before the winter "freeze-up" of the waters, and after the ice had broken up in the spring. However, the fall was a season of profitable buffalo hunting

[27] Clements and Shelford, 1939, pp. 20–24: "The biome or plant-animal formation is the basic community unit ... two *separate* communities, plant and animal, do not exist in the same area.... The plant-animal formation is composed of a plant matrix with the total number of included animals, of which the larger and more influent species may range over the entire area of the biome.... The extent and character of the biome are exemplified in the great landscape types of vegetation with their accompanying animals, such as grassland or steppe, tundra, desert, coniferous forest, deciduous forest, and the like...."

out on the Plains away from the haunts of the beaver, and a period when dried provisions had to be accumulated to last through the dead of winter. Likewise, by spring food supplies had been exhausted, so that it was imperative to pursue the bison on the Plains as soon and as diligently as possible, even though the hunting might be more successful later during the summer months. The prospects for winter beaver hunting were equally poor, though the camps might be scattered in Woodland localities, such as river valleys, the foothills of mountain ranges, or isolated ranges of hills, such as the Black Hills, for the beaver was then inaccessible. Another factor which inhibited the diffusion of beaver trapping in this area is that, like other Woodland animals, beaver could be hunted successfully only by small bands of hunters, or by individual hunters spread out over a wide area. Bison hunting, on the other hand, demanded many hunters and encouraged the concentration of a relatively large population in relatively permanent camps. The social and psychological adjustments to this latter condition of life became, in turn, a strong deterrent to any seasonal dispersion not absolutely forced by nature.

The above discussion indicates the reasons why the tribes of the Northwestern Plains did not produce the only commodity (i. e., beaver and similar furs) that could be exchanged for the guns and ammunition of the traders, and why the tribes therefore did not develop the Post-gun—Pre-horse or Horse *and* Gun military technique patterns at this time. As an illustration of this situation, Henry, in 1809, stated that the Plains Cree

...are fully as much addicted to spirituous liquors as the Saulteurs [i. e., Ojibwa], but generally have no means of obtaining it. Those only [i. e., of the Cree] who frequent the strong wood country[28] can purchase liquor and tobacco. Those who inhabit the Plains are a useless set of lazy fellows — a nuisance both to us and to their neighbors, and much addicted to horse stealing. They are generally found in large camps winter and summer, idle throughout the year.[29] Buffalo is their only object. Although passionately fond of liquor and tobacco, still they will not resort to the woods where they could procure furs to purchase those articles.[30] In winter they take to the bows and arrows; firearms are scarce among them, and they use but little ammunition...[31]

[28] A literal translation by Henry of the French name for a certain region of dense forest.

[29] "Idle" from the point of view of the industrious fur trader, since they did no hunting for beaver, etc.

[30] This would naturally also include guns and ammunition.

[31] Coues, 1897, vol. 2, p. 512.

CHAPTER FIVE

HORSE AND GUN PATTERN ON THE NORTHWESTERN PLAINS

"Occasional Gun Period"

The next phase in Plains warfare history occurred with the contact and interaction between the two military technique patterns, Post-horse—Pre-gun and Post-gun—Pre-horse, in the Northwestern Plains. This transitional state continued until their eventual synthesis into the so-called "Typical" form, Horse *and* Gun, of the mid-nineteenth century. With regard to its genesis, it may be noted that as early as the late 1730's, still the period of Pre-horse—Pre-gun warfare, a few guns were occasionally used in battle. With reference to the influence of the gun on warfare, we may call this the "Occasional Gun Period."

The original source of these guns was a group of Cree living in the marginal Plains region and in process of transition from adaptation for an exploitation of the Woodland aspect of their environment to an adaptation for an exploitation of the Plains aspect of their environment. As the process continued, these people gradually cut themselves off from their own source of supply of guns and ammunition because they ceased to hunt beaver, their only medium of exchange with the traders. Soon they were unable to provide even the few guns they occasionally traded with the Blackfoot for the latter's war with the Snake. Thus, according to Henry, the group of Cree who were living in a marginal Plains area in 1809 and becoming a true Plains people, now acquired few guns themselves, and "if they procure a gun it is instantly exchanged with an Assiniboine for a horse."[1] Taking all evidence into account, including Saukamappee's account of the second Snake-Blackfoot battle,[2] it is evident that, while the presence of even a few guns could be decisive in a massed infantry battle, the infrequency with which any guns at all were available prevented these weapons from modifying the military technique pattern. Furthermore, after the full development of mounted war, these same few guns exercised a much less potent effect, since their accuracy was much diminished by the rapid mobility of the target, particularly when they were fired from horseback rather than from afoot. It must also be noted that slowness

---

[1] *Ibid.*, p. 512.

[2] A battle by two opposing infantry lines, in which a few gun-equipped Cree fighting with the Blackfoot enabled them to win a decisive victory (Tyrrell 1916, pp. 330–332. See this paper, pp. 36–37).

of reloading, in conjunction with the extremely small numbers of guns ever present at any battle, made the fire extremely discontinuous, with long vacant intervals during which the mobility and rapid firing rate of the mounted archer could have effect. This was quite a different situation from that in which a fair proportion of the warriors were armed with guns. In the latter instance, the pauses caused by long reloading time could be avoided by an informal system of rotation which maintained a rather continuous fire. Thus, because of its scarcity, at this early period the gun was not an organizing factor in the development of the military technique pattern, while the horse, bow, lance,[3] and leather armor were. These latter factors interacted to produce the full Post-horse—Pre-gun military technique pattern which was in active existence in the Northwestern Plains until the mid-1780's, as the Umfreville account informs us. Referring to the people of the Plains, he states that

> Notwithstanding the warrior uses so much address to find his enemy unprepared, yet it sometimes happens that he is discovered, and a safe retreat becomes impracticable. In this dilema both parties fight with great bravery, each side being *provided with coats of mail made of many folds of drest leather,* which are impenetrable to the force of arrows: they have also shields, made of undrest Buffalo hides, which they shift about in the times of action with admirable dexterity and skill.... Their horses are of great service to the Indians in these expeditions, and are much esteemed by them...[4]

Again, illustrating the full Post-horse—Pre-gun military technique pattern on the Northwestern Plains, Lewis and Clark, speaking of the Shoshone, state that

> They have also a kind of armor which they form with many foalds of dressed a[n]telope's skin, unite with glue and sand. with this they cover their own bodies and those of their horses. these are sufficient against the effects of the arrow.[5]

Furthermore, a tradition of the use of the steel-tipped lance among the Shoshone is reported by a modern ethnographer.[6] Wissler also states that, although Maximilian in the mid-19th century saw few lances among the Blackfoot, his own information indicates that they were at one time in general use, and that this direct testimony is reinforced by the fact that the warrior societies used the lance as an important part of their regalia. In addition, he says that although wooden armor was unknown, there were "... traditions implying that buckskin shirts of two or more thicknesses were worn as protection against stone and bone points."[7] Finally, in 1772–73 Cocking traveled up the southern branch

---

[3] For a reference to the Shoshone use of the steel-tipped lance, see Lowie, 1924, p. 242.

[4] Umfreville, 1790, pp. 188–89. Italics FRS.

[5] Lewis and Clark, 1904–05, vol. 3, p. 21.

[6] Lowie, 1924, p. 242.

[7] Wissler, 1910, pp. 162–63.

of the Saskatchewan River into the Plains with a band of Cree who "showed me a Coat without sleeves six fold leather quilted, used by the Snake tribe to defend them against the arrows of their adversaries."[8] When in a Blackfoot camp he noticed that "They are all well mounted on light Sprightly animals; Their Weapons, Bows & Arrows: Several have on Jackets of Moose leather six fold, quilted, & without sleeves."[9]

During this "Occasional Gun Period," when the Post-horse—Pre-gun pattern was dominant, the threat of the Snake was sufficiently grave to force the establishment of a loose coalition among the Blackfoot, Sarsi, Atsina, Assiniboin, and Plains Cree. It is to be noted that each of these groups had the same relationship to the Snake. When the Assiniboin and Cree began adjusting their culture to the Plains type of biome they gradually moved further onto the Plains. Here they found themselves exposed to the Snake raids, to which they were now more vulnerable because of the decline in their supply of guns and their, as yet, inadequate supply of horses. Although the other tribes, closer to the Snake, were better supplied with horses, their needs were still far from filled. Since the Snake had more horses than all the other tribes, a declining gradient in the quantity of horses was formed, passing from the Snake to all the other Northwestern Plains tribes. This very steep gradient effectively oriented the horse-raiding activities of these latter tribes toward the Snake, and overrode any tendency for mutual horse-raiding within the group of allied tribes that the inter-tribal gradients of smaller intensity might have produced.

Furthermore, since the exchange value of captives had no relation to their particular tribal origin, the Snake raided indiscriminately. This reinforced the polarization of all surrounding tribes toward the Snake as *the* enemy. Since the hostility of this functionally defined group of tribes was focused on the Snake, the opportunities that existed for inter-tribal aggression were ignored. Tribes of this *de facto* alliance obtained horses from one another by trading rather than by raiding, so that the slight quantitative differences in the possession of horses and European trade goods that resulted from different locations on the two opposing gradients actually promoted friendly relations based on amicable exchange.

Since the Woodland Cree occupied a totally different position with regard to the relevant influences, they did not participate in this allied group and, indeed, continued to maintain hostile relations with all the Plains tribes as a result of their aggressive expansion, which stemmed from their relation to the fur trade. However, in the relationship of the Plains Cree to the Assinboin, the bonds of kinship and traditional alliance usually overcame this hostility.

[8] Burpee, 1909, p. 110.
[9] *Ibid.*, p. 111.

Reorganization of Fur Trade

In the decade following 1763, the date of the fall of New France, the whole situation in the Northwestern Plains began to change. The first result of the war and the French defeat in Canada had been a complete collapse of the fur trade from Montreal via the Great Lakes. However, the disappearance of the French government with its rigid control over the trade opened the way for a rush of small independent traders who, toward the end of this decade, were extending themselves to the north of the Saskatchewan, far beyond the greatest reach of the old French trade. Once consolidated into one group, the Northwest Company, they constituted an increasing threat to the trade of the Hudson's Bay Company, because of the effectiveness of coordinated effort, increased capital, and improved transportation by sailing ship on the Great Lakes.[10]

The most effective innovation of the Northwest Company in the far northwest was the substitution of Europeans for Indians in the function of collecting furs from the hunter and transporting them to the port of shipment to Europe. The French of the "Old Regime" had been attempting this, but were relatively unsuccessful for a variety of reasons, among which were the superiority of English manufactures over French, the sheer length and difficulty of the line of transportation, the inhibition of enterprise by rigid central control, and the failure to extend into and tap the vast fur resources of the Northern Forest region in the Mackenzie basin. The Hudson's Bay Company had always preferred using Indian middlemen to bring the furs to their seaside warehouses, as this system kept the personnel of the company, and hence the expenses, at a minimum. However, it was found that the Indians always preferred to exchange their furs for trade goods as near their home territory as possible, even at increased prices. The main reason for this was that the Indian hunting subsistence economy could not produce a surplus sufficient to maintain separate classes of individuals with specialized functions. Thus each individual was forced to allocate his available time among all necessary activities.

This lack of specialization necessarily made for a proportionate decrease in efficiency of performance, as the number of activities engaged in increased. Hence, the assumption of one of these activities by the Europeans was welcomed. They were especially happy to relinquish this particular activity because it involved long trips over great distances, which conflicted with the vital activities of warfare, and especially, hunting for food. It is to be noted that, from a short-term point of view, it was to the disadvantage of the Europeans to act as middlemen and to the advantage of the Indians, while just the opposite was true from a

[10] Innis, 1930b, p. 389.

long-range point of view, because the middleman had the greatest power to influence both producer and consumer.

Yet we may not attribute this shift to the fact that the Europeans possessed greater ability to look into the future than did the Indians. Rather, it was largely due to the geography of North America, which created two separate, major routes of water transportation into the fur-producing areas of the interior. One route was via Hudson Bay and the major rivers of its drainage basin, such as the Saskatchewan; the other was via the St. Lawrence and the Great Lakes, with an easy access to the basin of the Saskatchewan. These two separate avenues of approach strongly conditioned a tendency toward the development of at least two separate fur-trading organizations; and the existence of these two organizations led inevitably to competition in the regions where their expanding operations overlapped. The Northwest Company was the newcomer and, having reemployed the "coureur de bois," that basic element of the French fur transport system, it advanced the middleman function to service the Mackenzie basin, and thereby so cut into the rich trade of Hudson's Bay Company from that area that the latter was forced to adopt the same measure.

The immediate result of this changed situation in the Northwestern Forest area was that the Cree were displaced as middlemen, while the Athabascans, who had produced and been robbed of a large proportion of the furs from this area, now received a steady supply of guns and ammunition from the traders, which made them the equals in war of the Cree. At this point the advance of the Cree stopped abruptly, and the Athabascans even began to press them back in places.[11]

In order to support the manpower required to operate the trading posts and local expeditions, as well as to bring in trade goods and take out the furs over the great distances involved, it was necessary to make special provisions for the procuring of food. The transport specialists, the canoe men, could not live off the land by hunting, beyond a certain minimum degree, because the time and uncertainty involved in hunting would so reduce their rate of travel that they would be unable to cover the enormous distances to be traversed within the season of open water. Therefore, they had to take supplies with them. However, if the food supplies were too heavy and bulky it would reduce, below the margin of profit, the amount of trade goods or furs that could be carried in the limited canoe space. This forced the canoe men to carry only foods which had a maximum caloric content per unit of weight and volume, and which were non-perishable under the rough conditions of canoe travel.

Throughout the Great Lakes territory, during both the French and the British eras, the foods used were compact maize meal and the oil of animals, chiefly the bear. It was the specialized function of the inter-

[11] Franklin, 1823, p. 69; Mandelbaum, 1940, pp. 181–182.

mediate posts along the route to accumulate these supplies at the specified points by trade with the local horticultural and hunting Indians, and in addition, to raise some of their own supplies at better developed posts such as Machillimackinac.

When the Northwest Company extended their transport system into the Mackenzie basin they passed beyond the region of Indian horticulture at the Great Lakes, and the distance from this point to the Mackenzie country was so great that their men were not able to transport enough maize from the Great Lakes area to support themselves. The only solution for them, as well as for the Hudson's Bay Company whose base of operations lay far beyond the horticultural area, was the use of the mixture of dried meat and animal fat known as pemmican. However, the only region which had adequate animal resources together with the technique and organization for supplying pemmican in the required, regular amounts was the Plains. Thus, the region which had heretofore been devoid of interest to the fur trade suddenly attracted the interest of the commissariat of both companies.

Effect of Reorganization on Military Patterns

The fur companies gradually extended their posts and activities in this Northwestern Plains area during the last quarter of the 18th century and the first decade of the 19th.[12] Up until about 1812 the trade can be described as moderate in intensity. The companies' need for pemmican was not yet sufficient in volume to enable the Indians to satisfy completely their great need and desire for European goods by the exchange of this commodity. Partly as a result of competition between the two companies and partly as a necessary policy of maintaining friendly relations with the tribes, they traded to some extent for the less valuable hides of the wolf, bison, and so forth, which could easily be hunted in the normal course of Plains life.

Naturally, they traded for all of the beaver they could persuade the tribes to trap, but the amount was not large. Thus, in 1809, while speaking of the Blackfoot, Henry says that

...beaver are numerous, but they will not hunt them with any spirit, so that their principal produce is dried provisions, buffalo robes, wolves, foxes ,and other meadow skins, and furs of little value.[13]

Somewhat later, when differentiating among the various groups of Blackfoot, he states that

Painted Feather's band are the most civilized and well disposed toward us. The Cold band are notoriously a set of audacious villains. The Bloods are still worse,

---

[12] Innis, 1930b, pp. 389–90; Mackenzie, 1902, vol. 1, pp. XXI–LXXXIII, but especially pp. XXIX–LIII.
[13] Coues, 1897, vol. 2, pp. 529–30.

always inclined to mischief and murder. The Piegans are the most numerous and best disposed towards us of all the Indians in the plains. They also kill beaver.[14]

Thus, there were a few groups of Plains peoples who did hunt a fair amount of beaver, and these got on best with the traders. Again Henry states that

The trade with the Slaves[15] is of very little consequences to us. They kill scarcely any good furs; a beaver of their own hunt is seldom found among them.[16]

Finally, Henry gives an example of a tribe, which had recently shifted from an adjustment to the Woodland to an adjustment to the Plains, showing the difference this made in their trade relation. He says,

A band of Sarcees [i. e., Sarsi] arrived with provisions and a few beaver skins; ... Those Indians formerly killed a great quantity of beaver, and were accordingly much indulged by the traders. But of late they hunt very little and still expect us to treat them as before.[17]

"Few Guns Period"

These increasing contacts between the Northwestern Plains Indians and the European traders began to have an effect upon the Indian military technique pattern of the region by increasing the number of guns markedly beyond that prevailing in the preceding "Occasional Gun Period." This era of the rise of a new pattern might be termed the "Few Guns Period," as an indication of the extent to which the tribes were so equipped. The changes effected by the use of the new weapons were so significant that we may well regard this period as being especially important in the genesis of the mature Horse *and* Gun pattern. Though the number of guns in use was small, the fact that they were now consistently present in battle with a steady supply of ammunition initiated the mutual assimilation of the Post-gun—Pre-horse pattern and the Post-horse—Pre-gun pattern into the Horse *and* Gun pattern.

Effect of Horse and Gun Pattern on Balance of Power and Tactics:

The first important change resulting from this development was that the allied group of Plains tribes,[18] the Blackfoot, Atsina, Sarsi, Assiniboin, and Plains Cree, instead of merely holding their own with the Snake or being on the defensive, embarked on a powerful, successful offensive. The Blackfoot, because of their geographical position on the

[14] *Ibid.*, p. 530.
[15] In this case meaning the Blackfoot.
[16] Coues, 1897, vol. 2, p. 541.
[17] *Ibid.*, p. 575.
[18] From now on this block of loosely allied tribes will be referred to as the "Allied Tribes" or as the "Blackfoot and their allies."

frontier, were the most active. In one generation, approximately the thirty years from 1770 to 1800, they advanced west and southwest from the Eagle Hills to the Rocky Mountains and the upper Missouri River, defeating and evicting the Kutenai and Flathead as well as the Snake, none of whom had access to a source of guns. During this period the Kutenai, Flathead, and the Snake, after several disasterous experiences, soon learned to avoid any large-scale pitched battles with their gun-equipped enemies. For example, in 1809, when Thompson was west of the Rocky Mountains in the vicinity of the Spokane River he met a band of "Kullyspell" (i. e., Kalispell) Indians. He states that

> ... a very old Indian told me, when a young man he made a heavy war club, with which he felt himself confident of victory, they formed a very large party against the Peeagans [i. e., Piegan], and hoped for success, when for the first time their enemies had two Guns and every shot killed a Man, we could not stand this, and thought they brought bad spirits with [them] we all fled and hid ourselves in the Mountains, we were not allowed to remain quiet, and constant war parties now harassed us, destroyed the Men, Women, and Children of our Camps and took away our Horses and Mules...[19]

General avoidance of the pitched battle reduced conflict to an almost completely guerilla type of warfare in which large parties made surprise attacks on small camps. This development somewhat offset the advantages which the possession of guns gave the Blackfoot and their allies. As an example of the shift in tactics we cite Saukamappee's sequel to the second battle in which a few guns had given decisive victory to the Blackfoot:

> The terror of that battle and of our guns has prevented anymore general battles, and our wars have since been carried by ambuscade and surprize of small camps.... While we have these weapons [i. e., guns, iron arrowheads, knives, and axes], the Snake Indians have none, but what few they sometimes take from one of our small camps which they have destroyed, and they have no Traders among them. We thus continued to advance through the fine plains to the Stag River [Red Deer River]...[20]

By making sure of complete surprise and overwhelming numbers a Snake war party could count on victory, even though a few guns might be present in a small enemy camp. However, the Blackfoot tended to counter this tactic by remaining gathered in large camps which the Snake could never attack with success, even though such concentrations might be undesirable at certain seasons. Saukamappee states that

> ... the Snake Indians are no match for us [i. e., the Blackfoot]; they have no guns.... but they have the power to vex us and make us afraid for the small hunting parties that hunt the small deer for dresses and the Big Horn for the same and for Bowls. They keep us always on our guard.[21]

[19] Tyrrell, 1916, p. 463.
[20] *Ibid.*, pp. 335–336.
[21] *Ibid.*, p. 340.

Henry also says of the Blackfoot that "In summer they were obliged to assemble in large camps of from one hundred to two hundred tents, the better to defend themselves from enemies."[22]

In spite of the efforts the Snake made to avoid them, pitched battles occasionally occurred by accident. A large Snake camp might be surprised by a large Blackfoot force or a large Snake war-party discovered by a concentration of Blackfoot.

Some elements of the previous military technique patterns continued to survive during this period. Leather armor still fulfilled a vital function in engagements, since in each fighting force the vast majority of the warriors were armed only with the bow as a projectile weapon, though one side might, in addition, possess a few guns. Its use therefore continued, although diminishing in frequency of occurrence toward the end of this period. Moreover, it is evident that two alternative forms for the large-scale pitched battles existed. Though such battles were rare during the greater part of this period they occurred more frequently toward its close, when guns had spread to all the contending groups. One form was the cavalry battle typical of the Post-horse—Pre-gun military technique pattern, and the other was the battle by infantry lines, probably a survival of the still earlier Pre-horse—Pre-gun pattern.

To judge from Saukamappee's account of a second Snake-Blackfoot battle (see pp. 36–37) it would seem that this can be regarded as a transitional link. It is similar in form to the first Snake-Blackfoot battle which was clearly within the Pre-horse—Pre-gun pattern. Technically, however, it must be placed in the Post-horse—Post-gun period, because the Snake had the horse, although it was not used in this battle, and the Blackfoot had a few guns. Still, in spite of this, the scarcity of horses and guns produced a special situation in which the combatants were led to employ the old infantry-line formation. Later, when the supply of horses was plentiful and both sides had a few guns, a full cavalry battle might well have seemed advantageous to the attackers, and indeed have taken place, if both sides felt sure of victory or if one side surprised the other on horseback. However, if one side were less confident, it would probably have elected to employ the still existing and alternative formation of the infantry-line battle.

It seems likely that the Blackfoot were forced to retain the infantry line battle formation throughout the Post-horse—Pre-gun era, whenever their supply of horses was inadequate for a cavalry battle. However, there is no evidence that the Snake, who had a constant, large supply of horses during this same period, retained the earlier form. When the "Few Guns Period" arrived, the infantry battle pattern appears to have been established more firmly in those tribes which had access to guns, because fire from afoot was far more accurate than fire from horseback,

[22] Coues, 1897, p. 723.

and it was necessary to get the most efficient performance from the relatively few guns available.[23] This consideration was particularly im-portant for the force on the defensive. Hence, such a force would usually adopt the infantry pattern, even if the warriors were mounted before the battle. If the defensive force were not too inferior in numbers to the attackers, if they had chosen terrain impeding the movements of horses, and if they had a significant number of guns, the attacking group would be compelled to dismount and utilize the infantry tactics of their opponents to have any chance of defeating them. The battle between the Flathead and the Blackfoot in 1810 demonstrates this point: Thompson reports that

> The Saleesh [i. e., Flathead] Indians during the winter had traded upwards of twenty guns from me, with several hundreds of iron arrow heads, with which they thought themselves a fair match for the Peeagan [i. e., Piegan] Indians in battle on the Plains. In the month of July when the Bison Bulls are getting fat, they formed a camp of about one hundred and fifty men to hunt and make dried Provisions... they crossed the Mountains by a wide defile of easy passage, eastward of the Saleesh Lake, here they are watched by the Peeagans to prevent them hunting the Bison... they were determined to hunt boldly and try a battle with them: they were entering upon the grounds, when the scouts, as usual early each morning sent to view the country came riding at full speed, calling out, "the Enemy is on us;" instantly down went the Tents, and tent poles, which, with the Baggage formed a rude rampart; this was barely done, when a steady charge of cavalry came on them, but the Horses did not break through the rampart, part of pointed poles, each party discharged their arrows, which only wounded a few, none fell; a second, and third charge, was made; but in a weak manner; the battle was now to be of infantry. The Saleesh, about one hundred and Seventy men drew up and formed a rude line about four hundred yards from them; the Saleesh and the white men lay quiet on the defensive; the Peeagans, from time to time throughout the day, sent parties of about forty men forward, to draw them to battle; these would often approach to within sixty to eighty yards springing from the ground as high as they could, then close to the ground, now to the right, and to the left; in all postures; their war coats of leather hanging loose before them; their guns or bows and arrows, or a lance in their hands; the two former they sometimes discharged at their enemies with little effect: Buche, who was a good shot, said they were harder to hit than a goose on the wing. When these were tired they returned, and a fresh party came forward in like manner, and thus throughout the day ... the evening ended the battle; on the part of the Peeagans, seven killed and thirteen wounded; on the part of the Saleesh, five killed and nine wounded; each party took care of their dead and wounded; no scalps were taken.. This was the first time the Peeagans were in a manner defeated...[24]

Another eastward expedition of the Flathead and allied tribes in August of 1814 to battle again for the bison Plains further demonstrates this point:

> ... at the appointed time, a strong party was formed, and marched to the hunting of the Bison... the hunting was carried on with cautious boldness into

[23] Tyrrell, 1916, pp. 370–371.
[24] Ibid., pp. 423–25.

the lands of their enemies, this insult brought on a battle; the Saleesh and their allies had chosen their ground, on a grassy ridge with sloping ground behind it. Horses were not brought into action, but only used to watch each other's motions; the ground chosen gave the Saleesh a clear view of their enemies, and concealed their own numbers. The action was on the green plains, no Woods were near; the Peeagans and their allies cautiously advanced to the attack, their object being to ascertain the strength of their enemies before they ventured a general attack, for this purpose they made slight attacks on one part of the line, holding the rest in check, but no more force was employed against them than necessary, thus most of the day passed. At length in the afternoon a determination was taken to make a bold attack and try their numbers. Every preparation being made, they formed a single line of about three feet from each other, and advanced singing and dancing, the Saleesh saw the time was come to bring their whole force into line, but they did not quit their vantage ground; they also sung and danced their wild war dance; the Peeagans advanced to within about one hundred and fifty yards, the song and dance ceased, the wild war yell was given, and the rush forward; it was gallantly met, several were slain on each side, and three times as many wounded, and with difficulty the Peeagans carried off their dead and wounded and they accounted themselves defeated.... The combatants were about three hundred and fifty on each side...[25]

The Blackfoot and their allies, now victorious over the Snake, were still faced with the difficult problem of finding commodities the Europeans would accept in trade for guns and ammunition and learning how to secure these few types of goods. The market for pemmican was as yet quite small compared with the Indians' great need for guns, which they now recognized as essential for victory in war. Considering their specialized adaptation and commitment to full Plains life, the tribes had several possible ways in which to bridge the significant gap between felt need and effective economic demand. All of these they either employed or considered at various times.

In the first place, the companies were aware of this gap and knew that lack of satisfaction of the Indians' needs would inevitably lead to bad feelings and perhaps even to open hostility directed at their field representatives. In an attempt to narrow the gap they had authorized the purchase of limited numbers of hides of low value, such as wolf and bison hides, which were readily available to the Plains people. However, when the European fur market was glutted, they were tempted into the dangerous economy of prohibiting the purchase of these hides of little value. Under the urgency of one such occasion, the Atsina nearly put into action a plan to attack the trading post, kill the staff, and seize the needed guns by force. Thus, Henry learned from the Blackfoot that

... they were given to understand by the Fall Indians [i. e., Atsina] that it was the ill treatment they had received of late years from the traders at Fort Augustus; ... when they took in wolves to trade, one half, or three-fourths, and sometimes even the whole of the skins were kicked out of the fort, and they got

[25] *Ibid.*, pp. 551–52.

nothing for their trouble in killing them; while as for guns and ammunition, they could get none from the traders ... a party of them had just returned from war upon the Crows with whom they had fought a battle on the Yellow Stone River, where they had seen a fort which they supposed to be occupied by Americans.... In the heat of battle, the Crows called out that in future they would save the Fall Indians the trouble of coming to war, for next summer the Crows, in company with Americans, would go to war on the Saskatchewan. This information caused no little commotion and uneasiness among the Fall Indians. They knew their enemies were numerous and brave, and if headed by Americans, would carry all before them. Retreat would be in vain; the strong woods could not furnish animals enough for their support; ... destruction stared them in the face. They had but one resource — to enter our forts under pretense of. trade, take us unawares, murder us, and steal our property; which having done, they would be enabled to defend themselves against their enemies ...[26]

However, the Indians usually perceived that such actions would have undesirable consequences—permanent loss of access to guns—which would more than outweigh the short-term advantages to be gained.

Another alternative which the overwhelming power of their guns now allowed them to put into practice was the taking of captives for sale in the markets of Upper and Lower Canada.[27] With regard to this activity in the late 1780's Umfreville of the Hudson's Bay Company states that

On the other, or western side of the Stony Mountain are many nations of Indians, utterly unknown to us, except by Indian information.... All I can say for certain is, that a principal nation of these Indians is known to us by the name of the Snake Indians. That all the other Indians we have received an account of go to war against them every summer. In these war excursions many female slaves are taken, who are sold to the Canadian traders, and taken down to Canada ... and as for the captives they are rather happy in the change than otherwise; for if the conquerour had no prospect of making a profit by them, they would be all killed when taken...[28]

Incidentally, the superior military power of the Allied Tribes, which enabled them to take captives, at the same time virtually put a halt to this activity on the part of the Snake whose loss of this medium of exchange for their southern trade led to a definite impoverishment in their supply of European goods and weapons. This, in turn, accentuated the power disparity between them and the Allied Tribes. As Saukamappee points out

While we have these weapons [i. e., guns, iron shod arrows, knives and axes], the Snake Indians have none, but what few they sometimes take from one of our small camps which they have destroyed and they have no Traders among them.[29]

[26] Coues, 1897, vol. 2, pp. 719–20.
[27] Tyrrell, 1916, pp. 238–39; Dunn, J. P., 1905, p. 126; Wisconsin Historical Collection, 1910, vol. 19, p. 240.
[28] Umfreville, 1790, pp. 176–77.
[29] Tyrrell, 1916, p. 336.

Another way the Indians met the problem of insufficient purchasing power was through theft.[30] The articles that could be stolen most readily were small, plentiful, and not valuable enough for Europeans to carry constantly on their persons or lock up. Among them were metal objects, pieces of cloth, etc. But the items that the Indians needed most desperately, guns and ammunition, were, of course, highly valued and well guarded by the whites. As evidence of the Indian tendency to steal prized items whenever possible a source reports of the Blackfoot that

> They are notorious thieves; when we hear of a band coming in every piece of iron or other European article that can be carried off must be shut up. They have not yet begun to steal horses — no doubt because they have such vast numbers of their own.[31]

Another opportunity that was very often exploited was the need of isolated Europeans for sexual satisfaction. Here, the Indians made use of a commodity which they had readily available; they traded the sexual services of their women for limited periods. As Henry says,

> In their visits to our establishments women are articles of temporary barter with our men. For a few inches of twist tobacco a Gros Ventre will barter the person of a wife or daughter with as much sangfroid as he would bargain for a horse. He has no equal in such an affair, though the Blackfoot, Blood, or Piegan is now nearly as bad — in fact, all those tribes are a nuisance when they come to the forts with their women. They intrude upon every room and cabin in the place, followed by their women, and even though the trader may have a family of his own, they insist upon his doing them the charity of accepting of the company of at least one woman for the night. It is sometimes with greatest difficulty that we can get the fort clear of them in the evening and shut the gates; they hide in every corner, and all for the sake of gain, not from any regard for us ...[32]

When the foregoing methods proved inadequate, the Indians resorted to warfare and forcibly seized that prime medium of exchange, the beaver pelt, from their enemies. In 1809, a source reports of the Blackfoot that

> Last year, it is true, we got some beaver from them; but this was the spoils of war, they having fallen upon a party of Americans on the Missourie, stripped them of everything, and brought off a quantity of skins.[33]

However, this last technique did not expand into a major activity as it had among the Woodlands Cree and the tribes of the Northeastern Forest area, for the simple reason that their native enemies of the Plains hunted the beaver as little as they did themselves, and therefore had no supply of the valuable pelts. As a rule, war was a feasible solution

[30] Coues, 1897, vol. 2, p. 736.
[31] *Ibid.*, p. 526.
[32] *Ibid.*, p . 735.
[33] *Ibid.*, p. 541.

only when White trappers were present in the area and had exposed themselves to military defeat, as the quotation cited suggests.

The new military superiority of the Allied Tribes, and their subsequent victory over the Snake, had a variety of consequences, not the least of which was an increase in successful horse-raiding. The victories of the Allied Tribes also paved the way for the conquest of vast new bison hunting grounds, and the capture of women and children. These latter were of value not only for purposes of trade, but also through adoption, for population increase.

Of necessity, most of the horses captured in warfare accrued to the tribe occupying the frontier—the Blackfoot. Thus their geographic situation accounted for a marked gap between them and the other Allied Tribes on the horse gradient. Formerly, the greatest disparity had existed between the Snake, Flathead, and Kutenai, on the one hand, and all of the Allied Tribes, including the Blackfoot, on the other. The changed situation therefore created great tension, and a tendency for cleavage within the Allied Tribes developed. At the same time, the great cohesiveness, which the military threat of the Snake to all the tribes had induced, was nearly eliminated by the increased supply of guns. As a consequence, the former allies began to separate into two increasingly hostile and warring groups,[34] comprising the Blackfoot and their satellite tribes, the Sarsi and sometimes the Atsina, on one side, and the Plains Cree-Assiniboin combination, on the other.

This situation, with its resulting alignment of warring groups, persisted until the end of the native period on the Plains. The opinion the Blackfoot held of their "Allies" by 1813 is clearly expressed by a mission which visited the Flathead to try to make peace. "The Peeagans replied, 'Our Allies do more harm to us than to you, for on pretence of making an inroad on you, they often steal our Horses'".[35] This practice was not uncommon even earlier, according to Henry who, in 1809, referring to "The frequent disturbances between the Slaves [i. e., Blackfoot] and the Crees..." says, "The Crees have always been the aggressors in their disturbances with the Slaves..."[36]

It should be noted that the pressure of the victorious Allied Tribes was felt equally by both the Snake and the Kutenai-Flathead-Nez Percé group. In the period of Snake military domination which had just passed, the latter group of tribes had been victims of the Snake, and relations between the two groups of tribes had been exceedingly hostile. However, in the new warfare situation, the Kutenai-Flathead-Nez Percé coalition were once again victimized, this time by the Blackfoot and the other Allied Tribes. As a result, a tendency developed

[34] *Ibid.*, pp. 532–33.
[35] Tyrrell, 1916, p. 547.
[36] Coues, 1897, vol. 2, p. 540.

for the coalition to forget its old enmity and to ally itself with the Snake against the great new force that threatened them both. The Snake still had the greater herds of horses, which the Kutenai-Flathead-Nez Percé group coveted. Also, the Snake still needed captives to sell in the Southwest, and the Kutenai-Flathead-Nez Percé group remained their only possible source, since the Allied Tribes were now too powerful to be preyed upon.

The result of these conflicting relationships was a very unstable, loose alliance between the Snake and the Kutenai-Flathead-Nez Percé tribes. This situation is mentioned by Saukamappee when speaking of the expansion period of the Blackfoot and other Allied Tribes: "... the Snake Indians are a bad people, even their allies the Saleesh [i. e., Flathead] and Kootanaes cannot trust them, and do not camp with them..."[37]

In the final phase of the "Few Guns Period" there was a significant shift in the military balance of power in this region, initiated by the expansion of the area in which the European traveling traders and fixed trading posts operated beyond its previous boundaries toward the west. As a result of this expansion the tribes beyond the mountains and north of the Snake were now equipped with guns and ammunition in modest quantities which, however, proved sufficient to match the armament of their old enemies to the east. A change resulted immediately. Like the Blackfoot and the other Allied Tribes, once supplied with guns, the Western Tribes[38] shifted from the defensive to the offensive, and in a series of battles won back a section of the buffalo Plains for the summer hunt. After this initial eastward expansion, the Western Tribes settled into a military equilibrium with the Blackfoot and other eastern tribes with regard to territory, since both groups had the same degree of access to supplies of guns and ammunition. It is to be noted that, contrary to what has been previously stated,[39] the mere presence of guns did not rule out large-scale battles. Indeed, when the Western Tribes obtained guns, they deliberately courted such battles with the gun-equipped eastern tribes, in order to secure a military decision.[40] However, it is quite true that when only one side possessed guns, as was previously the case, the other side studiously avoided such battles, since the result could only be disaster for themselves.

Another interesting result of the acquisition of guns by the Western Tribes was that their loose alliance with the Snake immediately broke

---

[37] Tyrrell, 1916, p. 338.

[38] The term "Western Tribes" is used to refer to the loose alliance of the Kutenai, Flathead and Nez Percé.

[39] Lewis, Oscar, 1942, pp. 52–53.

[40] For illustration see the accounts given above (pp. 54–55) of battles between Flathead and Blackfoot fought in 1810 and 1814.

up. Since the Western Tribes could now hold their own against the Blackfoot and the other Allied Tribes, the motivation to unite with the Snake for mutual self-preservation was greatly weakened, and this allowed the previously coexisting hostile tendencies to dominate the relationship. For example, in the council which the Flathead held in 1814 to decide on a campaign against the Blackfoot, one leader said,

> We have suffered so much from those on the east side of the Mountains that we must now show ourselves to be men, and make ourselves respected, we shall muster strong, but although the Shawpatins [i. e., Nez Percé] are many and good Warriors, they cannot send many men to our assistance, as they are the frontier tribe on the south, and next to them is the great tribe of the Snake Indians ... who are their enemies.[41]

The final phase of warfare in this area was that of the full Horse *and* Gun period. The key factor in the intense development of this pattern was an increase in the number of guns from a supply sufficient to equip only a few men in each group to an arsenal capable of outfitting fifty percent or more of the warriors in the tribe. For example, Henry tells about a gathering of the Assiniboin for war, in 1809, and states that "These 880 tents might produce about 2,000 men capable of bearing arms....When all their firearms were collected and counted, the total was 1,100 guns..."[42]

The increase in the number of guns was due to a greatly increased demand for pemmican by the fur trade. Demand for this food developed as the fur trade began to expand northward in the Mackenzie basin and, especially after 1812, westward through the country beyond the Rockies to the Pacific. In addition, the transport system into the Northwest Plains area had developed to a point where traders no longer had to choose between bulky hides of little value and compact, highly valuable furs, but could ship out both in quantity. Thus, the fur trade in buffalo hides flourished for the first time and, together with the increased demand for pemmican, provided the Plains tribes with an abundance of items to exchange for guns, ammunition, and other European goods. Furthermore, the expansion of the fur trade led to an increase in European travel over the Plains, so that for the first time they had to buy a significant number of horses from the Indians.

The large numbers of guns in use by all contending groups during the period of the full Horse *and* Gun military technique pattern quickly made the old-style leather armor completely obsolete, since it did not give enough protection from the enemy to justify its complicated construction and heavy, cumbersome qualities. However, protection from the arrow was still desirable, since archery fire was occasionally en-

[41] Tyrrell, 1916, p. 551.
[42] Coues, 1897, vol. 2, p. 523.

countered, and sometimes a fairly large proportion of the foe was still equipped only with bows.

Since the shield would serve this purpose, although not as effectively as armor, and since it was light, small, easily handled, and easily manufactured, it was retained in the new era. In addition, the shield was also useful in warding off blows and thrusts when fire was replaced by shock in the course of a battle. Finally, another potent factor in the survival of the shield was that the shield was considered to be a locus of defensive magic. The latter belief became intensified during this period as a compensation for the great relative advantage offensive weapons had recently developed over defensive ones. Thus, the multiple defensive functions of the shield, combined with its relatively slight disadvantages as compared with full leather armor, made possible its persistence during the full Horse *and* Gun period. Since leather armor did not meet these qualifications it was doomed to extinction.

Effect of Horse and Gun Tactics on Distribution of Spanish Type Saddle

The tactics of the Post-horse—Pre-gun military technique pattern had maintained a fair balance between fire with the bow and shock with the lance. Since the gun now replaced the bow, to an extent limited only by the supply of the new weapons, it so greatly increased the effectiveness of fire power that shock became much less frequent, and the lance was no longer regularly used.

Decline of the lance produced a radical change in riding gear. The so-called "Spanish" type of saddle, with high pommel and cantle, was actually the saddle developed in Europe during the Middle Ages for the special requirements of the armored lancer, or "knight." The use of the lance as a primary weapon requires a saddle specially constructed to prevent the shock of impact from unseating the rider. The high pommel and cantle held the rider securely in place, although at the cost of his freedom of movement. Furthermore, the danger that the saddle itself would slip under the impact was avoided by securing it with two leather straps, one passing around the chest of the horse in front and the other passing under the tail in back. This type of riding gear had been brought from Europe by the Spaniards and, as a part of the Post-horse—Pre-gun military technique, had been carried toward the Northwest Plains, first by the Apache, and later by the Shoshone. Now that the presence of a large number of guns had caused the near elimination of the lance and had made shock subsidiary to fire, there was no longer sufficient need for this specialized type of saddle. It was replaced by a rather simple, stuffed leather pad type, closely resembling the "English" saddle of the more recent Northwestern Europeans.[43]

[43] For a description and for the method of construction of both the "old" and "new" types of saddles among the Blackfoot, see Coues, 1897, vol. 2, pp. 526–27.

The new saddle facilitated those remarkable acrobatic feats on horseback for which the Plains Indian of the late period was justly famed. A good example of these was the warrior's stunt of throwing himself forward to one side of the horse's neck and then shooting from underneath it. This custom gave some protection to the warrior from enemy fire, after he had been deprived of leather armor by the gun.

Although the discarded "Spanish" saddle now only hindered the freedom of movement of the warrior, its greater security and support still had value for the weaker or more burdened members of the society, such as the women, children, and old men. Thus it was widely retained as the "women's" saddle. It constitutes a good example of a culture "survival," an element which, in form, is clearly identifiable as characteristic of a previous period of that culture, but which has maintained itself by the acquisition or extension of a secondary function. These facts give added insight regarding Wissler's information on the distribution of the two types of saddles. According to Wissler, the "Spanish" type of saddle was "...almost exclusively confined to the Ute, Shoshone, Shahaptian, and Crow,"[44] though it also occurred in the mid-nineteenth century among the Navaho. These tribes occupied the extreme western and southern Plains, and were hence the furthest from the source of guns to north and east. It was therefore not surprising that they retained the old Post-horse—Pre-gun pattern along with certain of its elements, the lance and "Spanish" saddle, long after the developing Horse *and* Gun pattern had displaced them elsewhere on the Great Plains.

Decrease in Size of Military Formations

The introduction of the gun vastly increased the warrior's power to kill as well as the distance at which it could be done. The gun thereby apparently fostered a tendency for individualism in war as opposed to cooperative group action. However, since other factors prevented this tendency from developing to the extreme of the "one man army," it usually resulted in a decrease in the size of the fighting unit, in the degree of specialization of roles, and in the subordination to centralized control. At the same time, the extremely deadly effect of massed gunfire on concentrated, slow-moving military units completely eliminated the large-scale infantry form of battle.

The shift during the Horse *and* Gun period from the large war party to the small one, which Oscar Lewis demonstrated for the Blackfoot,[45] was, however, not due *only* to a plentiful supply of guns. The war potential of the contending groups was somewhat equalized by the

[44] Wissler, 1915*b*, p. 17.
[45] Lewis, Oscar, 1942, pp. 51–58, 59.

fact that *all* the tribes had a good supply of guns at this time, even the Snake now being in contact with American traders. Another factor which served to balance the forces was that the numerically weaker tribes were allied together, as in the case of the Flathead, Kutenai, and Sahaptin groups, and in that of the Sarsi, who adhered to the Blackfoot confederacy. On the basis of this "balance of power" situation, each of the groups had conquered and now continued to hold, at least seasonally, a section of the Bison Plains large enough for its needs. Hence, the desire for an increased food supply only obtainable by means of territorial expansion no longer served as a motivation for war. The increased opportunities for obtaining other articles desired by the white traders, which have been mentioned before, combined with a decline in the market for slaves, made raiding for captives both unnecessary and unprofitable.

Thus, another motive for war disappeared. The only remaining economic motivation was the continuing pressing demand for horses. Since the tactics best suited to this particular aim consisted of stealthy action by a few individuals acting as members of a loosely coordinated group, the new tendency for small fighting units, based on the presence of many guns, was thereby further reinforced. Because of the combination of factors here outlined the most prevalent pattern on the Northwestern Plains became one in which small, rather informal groups raided, mainly for horses. A secondary motive that developed out of these raids was the need to avenge the deaths of relatives, which often occurred on such expeditions.[46]

Under certain rather rare circumstances, such as the loss of a very important person or of a whole war party to the enemy forces, a tribe might institute a large-scale action, executed entirely by cavalry. The attacking force would attempt to surprise a sizable enemy camp and carry it by a sudden charge.[47] However, if the enemy were alerted, a more formal cavalry battle might occur between two opposing lines. In this situation the gun proved greatly superior to the bow, when enough warriors possessed guns so that an informal system of firing in rotation could develope. Such a system was necessary to compensate for the slow rate of fire of the single shot muzzle-loading gun. It is noteworthy that it was the slow firing speed of the Indian guns, together with the difficulty of hitting a rapidly moving target from horseback, that alone made these massed cavalry battles still feasible. Due to this, only a relatively low proportion of the fighters was ordinarily killed or injured.

The following quotation gives a dramatic example of a large-scale

[46] For a more detailed description of this small war party pattern, see Smith, M. W., 1938.

[47] Schultz, 1907, pp. 194–95.

action in the full Horse *and* Gun period. In this case, a surprise counter-attack resulted in a rout with heavy casualties. According to Rising Wolf,

... the Gros Ventre — then at war with the Blackfeet tribes — concluded a treaty with the Crows, and there was a great gathering of them all on lower Milk River, to celebrate the event. A party of young Gros Ventres returning from a raid against the Crees brought word that they had seen the Piegan camp in the Divide — or, as the whites called them, — Cypress Hills. This was great news .... What could the Piegans do against their combined forces ? Nothing. They would kill off the men, capture the women, seize the rich and varied property of the camp. So sure were they of success, that they had their women accompany them to sort out and care for the prospective plunder.

From a distant butte the war party had seen the Piegan camp, but had not discovered that just over a hill to the west of it, not half a mile further, the Bloods were encamped in force, some five thousand of them, or in all about one thousand fighting men .... One morning the Crows and Gros Ventres came trailing leisurely over the Plain toward the Piegan camp all decked out in their war costumes, the plumes of their war bonnets and the eagle fringe of their shields fluttering gaily in the wind. And with them came their women happily chattering, already rejoicing over the vast store of plunder they were going to possess that day. An early hunter from the Piegan camp, going with his woman after some meat he had killed the previous day, discovered the enemy while they were still a mile and more away, and hurried back to give the alarm, sending one of his women on to call out the Bloods. There was a great rush for horses, for weapons; some even managed to put on a war shirt or war bonnet. Luckily it was early in the morning and most of the horse herds, having been driven in to water, were feeding nearby. If a man did not at once see his own band, he roped and mounted the first good animal he came to. And thus it happened that when the attacking party came tearing over the little rise of ground just east of the camp they were met by such an overwhelming force of determined and well-mounted men that they turned and fled, firing but few shots. They were utterly panic-stricken; their only thought was to escape. Better mounted than their women, they left these defenceless ones to the mercy of the enemy, seeking only to escape themselves.

From the point of meeting a fearful slaughter began. Big Lake, Little Dog, Three Suns, and other chiefs kept shouting to their men to spare the women, but a few were killed before they could make their commands known. There was no mercy shown to the fleeing men, however; they were overtaken and shot, or brained with war clubs. So sudden had been the call that many men had found no time to select a swift horse, mounting anything they could rope, and these soon dropped out of the race; but the others kept on and on, mile after mile, killing all the men they overtook until their horses could run no more and their clubarms were well-nigh paralysed from striking so long and frequently. Few of the fleeing party made any resistance whatever, never turned to look backward, but bent forward in the saddle and plied the quirt until they were shot or clubbed from their seats. For miles the trail was strewn with the dead and dying, through which fled their women, shrieking with terror .... "Let them go," cried Big Lake, laughing. "Let them go! We will do as did Old Man with the rabbits, leave a few for to breed, so that their kind may not become wholly extinct."

A count was made of the dead. Only five of the Blackfeet had lost their lives, and a few been wounded. But along the trail ... three hundred Crows and Gros Ventres lay dead.[48]

[48] *Ibid.*, pp. 197–99.

CHAPTER SIX

HORSE AND GUN PATTERN ON THE NORTHEASTERN PLAINS

Early History

Our study of warfare in the Northeastern Plains will concentrate chiefly on the Sioux. Analysis of the Pre-gun—Pre-horse military technique pattern of this group must of necessity be incomplete, since there is little factual material on the Sioux during this period. It is evident, however, that there was occasionally intensive, large-scale fighting, with decisive results. It is also evident that the characteristic, specialized torture and cannibalistic patterns of the Northeastern Woodlands were entirely absent. This omission is emphasized in an account by Perrot, referring to the defeat of a Huron expedition by the Sioux in the mid-17th century. The author states that

> The [Huron] captives were conducted to the nearest [Sioux] village, where the people from all the others were assembled in order to share among them the prey. It must be observed that the Scioux, although they are as warlike or as crafty as the other tribes, are not like them, cannibals. They eat neither dogs nor human flesh; they are not even as cruel as the other savages, for they do not put to death the captives whom they take from their enemies, except when their own people are burned by the enemy. They were naturally indulgent, and are so now, for they send home the greater number of those whom they have captured. The usual torture which they inflict upon those whom they have doomed to death, is to fasten them to trees or stakes, and let their boys shoot arrows at them; neither the warriors nor any men, nor the women, took part in this. But, as soon as they saw their own people burned, they resolved to do the same by way of reprisal; even in this, however, they do not behave with as much cruelty as do their enemies — either because some motive of pity or compassion will not permit them to behold such suffering, or because they believe that only despair can make the captives sing during their torments with so much fortitude and bravery, if it may be so called. On this account they speedily kill their captives with clubs...[1]

The first contact of the Sioux with guns and other European metal goods occurred in the mid-17th century, as a result of their meetings with the eastern foes of the Iroquois, the Huron and Ottawa, who had fled to the western shores of the Great Lakes. The clear cultural separation which existed between the Western and Eastern Woodlands peoples was expressed, among other things, by their different attitudes toward crying. The Sioux had institutionalized crying as the most honorable manner of greeting people, while the eastern tribes regarded it as a final loss of manhood and a weakness that they tried not to give way to, even under torture by the enemy. Consequently, in their first period of con-

[1] Blair, 1911, vol. 1, pp. 168–170.

tact, the Huron and Ottawa regarded the Sioux as a cowardly, weak people, a notion which later military contacts painfully contradicted. Thus, in speaking of the first contact of the Sioux and Ottawa, Perrot states that

> All those villages [i. e., Sioux] sent deputies to those of the Outaoüas [i. e., Ottawa]; as soon as they arrived there, they began, according to their custom, to weep over every person they met, in order to manifest the lively joy which they felt in meeting them; and they entreated the strangers to have pity on them, and to share with them that iron, which they regarded as a divinity. The Outaoüas, seeing these people weeping over all who approached them, began to feel contempt for them, and regarded them as people far inferior to themselves, and as incapable even of waging war.[2]

The Sioux, at this time, were completely unacquainted with the fur trade, and when they hunted the beaver at all they did so mainly for the meat. However, the Ottawa and Huron effectively introduced them to the fur trade, in which these tribes were intermediaries between the eastern traders and the tribes of the west. The Sioux became excellent beaver hunters, being motivated by their desire to obtain guns and other metal equipment from the Ottawa and Huron in return for beaver pelts.

During this period, the Sioux lived mainly in scattered villages throughout the lake-studded woodlands of northern and eastern Minnesota. They practiced a mixed economy consisting of horticulture, hunting, and wild rice gathering. Seasonally, many of the groups made bison-hunting expeditions out on the adjacent prairie lands.

Advancing Gun Frontier and the Balance of Power

In the prolonged wars of the mid-17th century between the Sioux and the Cree-Assiniboin alliance, the Sioux were at first successful, probably because they possessed a few guns while their enemies had none. However, after the establishment of the Hudson's Bay trading posts in the 1670's the tide turned; guns and ammunition flooded the enemy's country, and almost every Cree and Assiniboin warrior could be so armed. Since both opposing groups lived in a rich beaver country and both knew about guns, the outcome of the war depended largely on the relative efficiency of the two supply lines.

Many factors prevented the Sioux from obtaining as many guns as their enemies. The Cree and Assiniboin had direct contact with the European trading posts on Hudson Bay, and these, in turn, were supplied directly from Europe by large seagoing vessels which could easily and quickly transport large quantities of any sort of goods. On the other hand, the Sioux were in contact with the European trading posts on the lower St. Lawrence River only through Indian middlemen whose

[2] *Ibid.*, p. 160.

sole means of transport over vast distances was the canoe, and who, for this reason and with great effort, could only carry a small amount of goods. Frequently also, the activities of the Iroquois partially or totally cut off the route, making the supply intermittent. Moreover, in the early phase, the trade monopoly the Huron and Ottawa enjoyed enabled them to exploit the urgent needs of the Sioux. They obtained all the beaver they needed to meet their own exchange requirements by trading only pots, knives, hatchets, and cheap baubles, but did not part with their own precious guns and ammunition. Last, but not least, because of the recurrent hostility between the Sioux and the immigrant eastern tribes, the latter were disposed to give the Sioux as few guns as possible during the periods of peace and trade.

The military position of the Sioux changed for the better in the next decade. By the 1680's the French were taking over the middleman function in the fur trade as far west as the Sioux country. They insured a fairly constant flow of trade by holding the Iroquois in check. The French also greatly increased the volume of trade the Sioux could carry on by replacing the generally hostile, neighboring eastern tribes as middlemen, thereby eliminating the near embargo on the sale of guns and ammunition to the Sioux.

The Sioux as Carriers

This improvement in their supply of weapons enabled the Sioux to block the further advance of their enemies. However, northern groups of Sioux, later known as the Teton and Yanktoni, had already been driven to the southern and western section of the Minnesota region, the prairie country, where they had taken up a new mode of life, abandoning horticulture completely.[3] Bison hunting on the prairie thus came to be most important and the dominating, organizing influence in their culture, though formerly it had played a minor role. These tribes now spent the warmer half of the year on the prairie hunting bison on foot. They carried their baggage and small skin tipis by dog travois and on the backs of their women. In the cold season they moved north and east into the margin of the forest land where they found plenty of firewood and shelter. Here they hunted the forest game, killing mainly the deer for food and mainly the beaver for pelts. In the spring they took their furs to the French posts to trade and then moved out on the prairies. Thus, from the 1680's to the 1760's, these Sioux lived a true Plains nomadic hunting life in summer and fall, except for the fact that, although they were well equipped with guns, they had no horses.

The Post-gun—Pre-horse military technique pattern of the Sioux appears to have been essentially the same as that of the tribes of the

[3] For a detailed account of this movement, see Hyde, 1937, pp. 6–12.

Northeastern Woodlands area with respect to the size of the fighting force, their arms, means of transportation, and method of battle. Although there were undoubtedly small-scale war parties, the most effective instrument was the large war party, consisting of several hundred men at least. These warriors were recruited from a number of bands, met according to prearranged plans, and set out against some enemy village about once a year in the summer season.

The warriors were nearly all armed with guns and traveled either on foot or, when the rivers favored their purpose, by birch-bark canoe. They appear to have had no knowledge of the type of battle fought between two opposing lines of infantry, such as has been described for the Northwestern Plains.[4] Their tactics were organized entirely with reference to a forest environment and conditioned by their weapons. Since they depended almost exclusively on firepower and since the gun had such a long-range and great penetrating power, they found it most expedient to scatter their forces so that the individual warriors could take advantage of the best nearby cover and still effectively support each other by fire.

This tactic was quite different from that imposed by the use of shock weapons, such as the war club. Warriors using the latter type of weapon could only obtain mutual support through close and regular formations. The advantage which open terrain affords for the use of fire weapons in the form of exposing the enemy to clear view is largely negated by its exposure of the fighter to the counterfire of the enemy. Moreover, this disadvantage of open terrain for the use of fire is added to by the increased mobility it confers on the enemy, allowing him to scatter his forces widely and keep them in movement, thus providing a very poor target for the fire weapons. Finally, if the enemy is armed with shock weapons, this increased mobility will be a great advantage to him and enable him to crush a widely scattered formation of fire weapon fighters, by effecting sudden concentrations of force on a fraction of the opposing side and destroying it bit by bit. Thus, to compensate for the disadvantages of open terrain a closer formation which will increase the density of fire is required.

An illustration of the effects of terrain plus choice of weapons on military tactics is found in the following quotation from La Hontan, which deals with the Iroquois during the 1680's:

> The Iroquois have this advantage over their enemies, that they are all armed with good firelocks; whereas the others, who use these engines only for the shooting of beasts, have not above half their number provided with them ...[5] The Iroquois are not so sprightly as most of their enemies, nor so happy in fighting with clubs; and it is for that reason that they never march but in numerous bodies,

---

[4] See this monograph, pp. 36–37, 54–55.
[5] La Hontan, 1905, vol. 2, p. 501.

and that, by slower marches than those of the other savages ....[6] The strength
of the Iroquois lies in engaging with firearms in a forest; for they shoot very
dexterously; besides that they are very well-versed in making the best advantage
of everything, by covering themselves with trees, behind which they stand stock-
still after they have discharged, though their enemies be twice their number. But
in regard that they are more clumsy and not so clever as the more southern
Americans they have no dexterity in handling a club; and thus it comes to pass
that they are always worsted in open field, where the clubs are the only weapons;
for which reason they avoid any engagement in meadows or open fields as much
as possible ...[7]

Thus, the Sioux introduced an essentially Woodland military technique pattern to the Plains, maintaining no regular formation and
keeping only close enough together to support one another. When they
were hard pressed they retreated to the nearest available patch of woods,
where they could employ their particular form of warfare to best
advantage. For instance, in the 1730's, in the war between the Cree and
Prairie Sioux, an expedition of

... 500 Cree after twenty day's march in the prairies came within sight of the
smoke of the village which they wished to attack at sunrise .... when their
rearguard was attacked by 30 Sioux who had crossed their track and who took
them for Assiniboin not on the warpath. The assailants killed four, when the
whole party came on them. The Sioux, surprised at the number of the enemy,
took flight, abandoning a portion of their arms, in order to reach an isolated wood
in the midst of the prairie, where the fight went on until nightfall, the Cree in the
open like brave men, the Sioux hiding behind trees.[8]

When, toward the middle-18th century, the Sioux began encountering
cavalry among their enemies, as among the Missouri village tribes, they
were able to hold their own by virtue of their guns and the numerical
strength of their warparties marshalled into irregular massed groups.

Gun Frontier Crosses Ecological Boundary

The reader may well wonder why the ecological boundary between
Forest and Plains was an effective barrier to the diffusion of the Post-gun—
Pre-horse military technique pattern onto the Northwestern Plains, but
not onto the Northeastern Plains. One must note that there are certain
types of determining factors that have an effect only when in combination with another specific determining factor. In this particular case
the presence in the northwestern area of the Indian as middleman in the
fur trade made the ecological boundary a barrier, while the presence of
the European as middleman in the fur trade of the northeastern area
left it only a boundary.

[6] *Ibid.*, p. 498.
[7] *Ibid.*, p. 497.
[8] Burpee, 1927, p. 136.

In the northwest the flow of guns stopped almost entirely at the forest margin. Since the Indian middlemen acted not only as traders but also as major participants in the tribal wars, they usually prohibited or effectively restricted the sale of guns and ammunition to their present or future enemies. With trade access to the vital guns and ammunition largely cut off, the remaining items which the Indian middlemen freely offered proved, for tribes that were completely adjusted to Plains life, to be an insufficient incentive to readapt to a more completely Woodland life in order to procure beaver for the fur trade. In addition, the Indian middlemen, who had the gun and the Post-gun—Pre-horse military technique pattern in the Forest region, did not themselves bring this pattern onto the Plains, because the difference between the Plains and the Forest environments was so great that it allowed no compromise in adaptation to persist for long.

This difference soon forced any marginal group to make a choice between the two. If a group of Indian middlemen chose the Plains, they inevitably lost their position in the fur trade, and hence, lost nearly all access to the guns and ammunition necessary to implement the Post-gun—Pre-horse military technique pattern. Had they attempted to combine adaptation to the Plains and the Woodlands in one annual cycle, they would have had to expend vast amounts of physical energy in the process, and psychological energy also, in adjusting to constant and necessary shifts in behavior. For example, the technique of canoe-making and handling might easily be forgotten after a brief period of full Plains life, while the long summer canoe voyage to the European trading posts and back left little time to devote to the best bison hunting season. Moreover, bison hunting conflicted with beaver hunting. Thus it was that, until the European middleman ousted the Indian in the northwest, the gun did not cross the ecological boundary in significant numbers, and the Northwestern Plains remained completely dominated by the Post-horse—Pre-gun military technique pattern. The Post-gun—Pre-horse pattern continued to be confined to the forest land to the north. However, in the northeast the European middleman had already replaced the Indian middleman before the horse and the Post-horse—Pre-gun military technique pattern arrived in the Northeastern Plains. Since the European trader was, in general, not a party to the tribal wars, he sold to all who had beaver. He thus provided a powerful incentive for Plains peoples to include a Woodlands phase in their annual economic cycle. At the same time, this addition was much less of a burden because it only meant *hunting* the Woodlands fauna. The tribes did not need to retain a mastery of canoe-building and navigation in order to trade at far distant posts, since the European trader transported the furs and brought the trade goods very near to the tribal territory. Thus, in the Northeastern Plains, guns were available at an earlier period, and the

Post-gun—Pre-horse military technique pattern flowed unimpeded out onto the Plains and occupied a considerable area before the horse and the Post-horse—Pre-gun pattern arrived there.

Effects of Siouan Expansion on War and Trade

During this entire Post-gun—Pre-horse phase the Prairie Sioux were waging war with two different types of enemies. The more formidable were their old Northern Forest opponents, the Cree and Assiniboin, some of whom were now becoming Plains people like themselves. The original stimulus of this war appears to have been ambition for increase in land, motivated by the needs of the fur trade. The war was kept going partially by the ever-recurring need for revenge. Since their enemies had guns and always came down out of the Northern Woodland, their type of warfare was of the Woodland variety. As a result, the Sioux responded with their former Woodland military technique pattern, which was thereby reinforced. It was this war which drove the Cheyenne west of the Missouri, since they were caught between the contending forces.

The other type of enemy was the sedentary horticultural hunting tribes who were the original inhabitants of the prairie lands of southwestern Minnesota, northern Iowa, and the easternmost Dakotas. These peoples, the Iowa, Oto, and Cheyenne among them, were totally without guns in the early part of this period, and had an inferior supply until near its end. Since they were also completely without horses until toward the end of the period, they were nearly defenseless against the Post-gun—Pre-horse military technique pattern of the Sioux.

The Sioux probably had two motives for war upon the horticulturalists, besides ever-present desires for revenge and personal prestige. The first, as recent immigrants into this area, was their fundamental need for bison hunting territory, all of which was previously occupied; the second was raiding for captives, an activity which has not as yet been documented for these people, but which can be legitimately inferred from evidence on neighboring tribes.[9] For instance, we have direct evidence that the Illinois, the southeastern neighbors of the Sioux, as soon as they got guns raided to the west against the Pre-horse—Pre-gun Pawnee and surrounding tribes for captives which they sold for European goods;[10]

[9] "Grignon's Recollections," Wisconsin Historical Collection, 1857, vol. 3, p. 256. Also, on Indian slavery see Smith, T. W., 1896–98, pp. 3–4; Dunn, J. P., 1905, pp. 25, 126, 128; Hamilton, 1898, p. 26; Lauber, 1913; "J. V.", 1858, pp. 1–63.

[10] "They [i. e., Illinois] are well-formed, nimble, and very adroit in using the bow and arrow. They use guns also, which they buy of our Indian allies who trade with the French; they use them especially to terrify their enemies by the noise and smoke, the others lying too far to the west, have never seen them, and do not

and it seems most unlikely that the Sioux refrained from using military superiority to take their gunless adversaries captive. Undoubtedly, a severe shortage of commodities of exchange soon developed; and since the Sioux had extended their range out onto the Prairie, the more time they spent hunting the bison the more difficult it became to devote enough time to hunting the beaver so that it *alone* might suffice to exchange for the guns, ammunition, and other European goods which they needed so badly. Buffalo hides were little desired by the Europeans at this time, but captives were valuable. Thus, raiding for captives could have become an important economic adjunct which, unlike beaver hunting, did not interfere with a progressive adaptation to Plains life.

Temporary Military Equilibrium Established

In the course of the wars the Sioux drove the Iowa and Oto from east to west as far as the Missouri. There they attacked them again, as well as the Omaha and the Arikara.[11] However, toward the close of this period, in the mid-18th century, the influence of several factors brought the Sioux and the Missouri village tribes into a relative military equilibrium. One factor was the eastward advance of the Horse Frontier. Enough horses now reached the village tribes to enable them to take over the Post-horse—Pre-gun military technique pattern of the tribes to the west and south. Furthermore, from trade with the Kiowa they obtained some metal weapons and other goods which came from the Spanish Southwest. Thus equipped, the mobility and rapid rate of fire of the mounted archer offset, to some extent, the advantage of the gun-equipped Sioux infantry in the open field. At the same time, the art of village fortification, long in existence, had been developed to high efficiency in defense against both the gun-equipped northeastern peoples and the horse-riding southwestern ones. Every feature of these villages, the choice of site, their large populations, their encircling broad moats, earth and palisade ramparts, and the very construction and arrangement of the houses was a result of the dominating idea of defense. For instance, when Thompson was visiting the Mandan in the winter of 1797–98,

> They enquired how we built our houses, as they saw me attentively examining the structure of theirs; when informed; and drawing a rough plan of our Villages, with Streets parallel to each other, and cross Streets at right angles, after looking at it for some time; they shook their heads, and said, In these straight Streets

know their use. They are warlike and formidable to distant nations in the south and west, where they go to carry off slaves, selling them at a high price to other nations for goods." (French, 1852, vol. 4, p. 32, from the "Relation of the Voyages, Discoveries, and Death of Father James Marquette, and the Subsequent Voyages of Father Claudius Allouez," by Father Claudius Dablon, 1678).

[11] Hyde, 1937, pp. 14–15.

we see no advantage the inhabitants have over their enemies. The whole of their bodies are exposed, and the houses can be set on fire; which our houses cannot be, for the earth cannot burn; our houses being round shelter us except when we fire down on them, and we are high above them; the enemies have never been able to hurt us when we are in our Villages; and it is only when we are absent on large hunting parties that we have suffered; and which we shall not do again. The Sioux Indians have several times on a dark and stormy night set fire to the stockade, but this had no effect on the houses ...[12]

Another factor that enabled the village tribes to meet the threat of the Sioux was that a northern supply-line[13] for guns and ammunition opened up. The quantities of these were small until the 19th century. The Assiniboin were the main link in this northern trade and brought European trade goods to exchange for maize and various Plains products.[14] Not enough guns and ammunition were obtained in this way to have much effect on the well-equipped Sioux in the open field, but when they were used from behind well prepared defensive works they were very effective and added greatly to the strength of these works.[15] The Sioux always tried to interfere with this trade with the Missouri village tribes, not only because they were the enemies of the Assiniboin, but also because they recognized the threat to their own progress that would result if the village tribes were well provided with European weapons.

A final factor which tended to maintain the military balance in this period was the notable diminution in the Sioux' supply of guns and ammunition. This was due to the collapse of the fur trade during the Seven Year's War, 1756–63, and afterwards, until about 1770, when independent traders reestablished the trade. The tribe's loss of arms was enough to offset their gains through the acquisition of horses during the same period.

Siouan Expansion Renewed

During this phase of the military balance of power, from around 1750 to 1770, the Sioux got their first horses from the Arikara, according to tradition, and began to develope horse nomadism and cavalry warfare. However, they were not well supplied with horses until some time after 1775.

It was here that the Post-gun—Pre-horse and Post-horse—Pre-gun military technique patterns were successfully synthesized into the complete Horse *and* Gun pattern with which the Sioux later swept on

[12] Tyrrell, 1916, p. 229.
[13] See Jablow, 1951, passim.
[14] Burpee, 1927, p. 228.
[15] The fortification of these upper Missouri villages had been very intense at an early period. Even bastions were a pre-contact feature. Their function was to allow a crossfire to sweep the intervening face of the main palisade for added support. Guns increased the efficiency of this function. See Strong, 1940, p. 382.

west and south across much of the northern and central Plains. The Sioux warriors selected those elements from each of the two patterns that were most useful to them. They retained their guns, of course, and used them as fully as the supply from trade then permitted. From the Post-horse—Pre-gun pattern they adopted the horse, with saddle, bridle, and stirrups for use in battle. They also adopted the lance and short bow as alternative weapons to be employed when they lacked guns and ammunition due to an unfavorable trade situation. Only part of the defensive equipment of the Post-horse—Pre-gun pattern was adopted. They did not bother with the complete leather armor, since it afforded too little protection against the gun to be worth the effort of manufacturing and wearing it. They did, however, incorporate some of the protective devices of the Post-horse—Pre-gun military technique pattern.

For example, the small, round leather shield and an attenuated form of the leather cuirass, or jacket,[16] were adopted. The reason for this particular selection was that the foes of the Sioux on the west and south still lacked guns, and hence used bows during this early period, so that these elements of the leather armor complex still had defensive value in battle against them.

At a later date, when the Gun Frontier had passed entirely beyond the Sioux, leaving them completely surrounded by gun-equipped tribes, the leather jacket lost most of its protective value. However, the acquisition of a secondary function entirely unrelated to defense determined its retention in a modified form. It became the symbol of a high-ranking office, that of "Shirt Wearer,"[17] and persisted in a single-layered, decorated form.

Shortly after 1770 a series of changes began which upset the balance of power, enabling the Sioux to expand westward. These changes were due to two circumstances. One was the renewal of the fur trade from Montreal, with the consequent increase in supplies of guns and ammunition. The other was the reduction of the population of the village tribes by about four-fifths, resulting from three epidemics of smallpox, in 1772–1780. Under strong pressure, the now greatly weakened Arikara moved northward, thereby opening a permanent road for the Sioux across the Missouri.[18]

The Sioux took advantage of this to cross to the west side in summer to hunt the buffalo, and to secure horses from the western tribes, mainly by raiding. In the fall they returned to their woodland camp sites to

---

[16] "... a garment like an outside vest with sleves that cum down to thare elboes made of soft skins and several thicknesses that will turn an arrow at a distans — and a target two and a half feet in diameter of the same material and thickness ..." (Innis, 1930a, p. 58).

[17] Wissler, 1912, p. 7.

[18] For a good account of the westward expansion of the Sioux, see Hyde, 1937, pp. 9–19, 20–42, 46, 52, 85–98.

hunt beaver, and in the spring they attended to trading for European goods. However, as they went further west of the Missouri and spent more time there, the necessary supply of guns and ammunition became more difficult to maintain. In the first place, the distance back east to the trading zone was great; in the second place, the increased specialization to a bison-hunting Plains life which was brought about by a full supply of horses made the diversion of time and energy to the Woodlands speciality of trapping beaver increasingly difficult and distasteful. In this situation, the extension of trading activities up the Missouri from St. Louis proved a great boon. The river provided an excellent, direct mode of transportation which made it possible to trade for bulky items, such as buffalo robes, deer skins, bear hides, buffalo tongues and tallow, as well as the compact, highly valuable beaver pelts. These products could be floated to market by bull-boat and canoe, later, by keelboat, and finally by steamboat. Once this expanding new market had entirely replaced their old trade route to the east via the Great Lakes, the Sioux were assured of an excellent supply of guns and ammunition. Since direct trade contact did not reach the western tribes until a number of decades later, the Sioux enjoyed a strong military superiority that greatly facilitated their expansionist tendencies.

At this time Indian captives ceased to be valued by the traders as a commodity of exchange because of the great new sources of manpower in the European settlements, and trade for Indian slaves came to a halt throughout the Northern Plains. However, the simultaneous rise of an increased market for products of the bison hunt more than compensated for the loss, and in the new period, the main purpose for the Sioux wars against the western tribes was to secure the essentials for the mounted, bison-hunting Plains life. The tribes needed horses and hunting grounds sufficient to support a population that was growing rapidly, both because of a high birth rate and the westward migrations of Sioux groups from east of the Missouri.

When Sioux expansion was resumed, the region around the Black Hills was occupied by the Crow on the north, the Cheyenne and Arapaho on the east, and the Kiowa on the south. These tribes were all desperately trying to equip themselves with guns. Their only sources of supply were the village tribes that had limited but important trade contacts with the British and with the Assiniboin to the north who traded with the British. The western tribes brought in horses, dried meat, and buffalo robes to exchange for maize and for guns, ammunition and other European goods. The Sioux intercepted this trade whenever possible, in order to prevent their western enemies from becoming well equipped with fire-arms.

The Sioux fought with the Arikara who held the west bank of the Missouri to the north of them, and the Omaha and Ponca who held the same position on the south. They also fought the Cheyenne and, in the course of this war, in 1794, surprised and captured the camp of a whole Cheyenne band. Soon after, the Sioux-Cheyenne war was ended by an alliance. The Kiowa were cut off from their trade with the Arikara and driven south, away from the Black Hills.[19] Serious war with the Crow began in 1785; they were forced west, away from the Black Hills and beyond Powder River.

During this period, horse-raiding was carried on by small, rather informal war parties, while effective domination of a particular territory was established and maintained by formal, large-scale actions which were organized in two distinct ways among the Sioux. In one case, the process might be initiated by a disaster to a war party or the death of a very prominent man. Following the bad news, the people waited one winter, during which time the relatives of the dead men took the war pipe to other camps where they publicly mourned their dead and asked for help. When the chiefs accepted and smoked the pipe, it was a pledge to join them. In the following summer, all the participating camps assembled and moved secretly, directly into enemy country, scouting for a camp. Finding one, they made camp and left the women, children, and old men. The warriors advanced by night and at dawn attacked, taking the camp completely by surprise, killing all except the young women and children, and capturing all the possessions of the enemy.

Other events leading up to a large-scale attack occurred when the bands came together in the summer toward the end of the bison hunt for the annual Sun Dance. At the end of this ceremony, a war party of several hundred warriors or more would set forth to deliver a heavy blow. If the enemy had not been surprised, and had had some time to prepare, then a large-scale, formal cavalry battle between two opposing lines took place. The battle might last for hours, or for most of the day, or it might be decided very quickly. The actual collision of the two lines was usually preceded by a period of indeterminate length, in which the warriors sang war songs and taunted the enemy, and their champions challenged and fought individual contests. It was customary, at this time, for daring warriors to ride the full length of the enemy line within range of enemy fire, taunting them and dodging their projectiles. Thus, according to an eye-witness account of a battle between Sioux and Crow on the Yellowstone River in 1873,

Alternate charging by Crows and by Sioux occupied the first hour of combat . . . the Crow warriors began riding the daring-line . . . . Man after man would gallop his horse along in front of the array of Sioux, shielding himself as best he could by riding on the animal's side while the enemy sent bullets and arrows toward him. Then the Sioux in their turn would give us a return game of the same kind . . .

19 Mooney, 1895–96, pp. 157–160.

The dares on foot began to be put into operation. An Indian of first one side and then the other would walk toward the enemy, would take his position on some little eminence and utter defiant or tantalizing remarks.[20]

In addition to the large cavalry war parties, well equipped with guns derived from a privileged trading position, there was another factor in Sioux success. This was the fact that they constituted a block of allied bands and tribes larger by far in population and area than any of their opponents. Thus, it was easier for the Sioux to gather large expeditionary forces together, and greater numbers were always an advantage in those cavalry battles in which both sides had a relatively similar type of equipment. From the standpoint of defense, their position was advantageous in that every tribe or group of bands in the Sioux alliance was at least partly surrounded by groups which would never attack it, and which served as a barrier against enemy forces. In contrast, the enemy tribes were relatively small and usually isolated or allied with only one other small tribe, so that they were subject to attack at any time from any direction. Assuming several enemy groups to be equally involved in a state of war, it is obvious that the smaller group would be under a greater relative stress.

After the termination of the War of 1812, and coincident with the introduction of steam navigation, the rapid expansion of intensive American trading activity along the whole length of the Missouri and through the entire west, by its very extension, eliminated the Gun Frontier, and largely obliterated even any gun supply gradients in the whole Plains area. Thus, the full Horse *and* Gun pattern of military technique spread west and south far beyond the Sioux, and the various later expansions of the Sioux were due, for the most part, to factors other than a greatly superior firepower over their enemies.

[20] Marquis, 1928, pp. 91–92.

CHAPTER SEVEN

HORSE AND GUN PATTERN ON THE SOUTHERN PLAINS

Returning, at last, to the Southern Plains, we shall seek to trace the advance of the Gun Frontier across this area from east to west. This task involves a study of the advance of the Horse *and* Gun military technique pattern, since the Post-horse—Pre-gun pattern had spread nearly to the eastern limits of the Southern Plains before the gun reached this section.

Political and Economic Basis for Advance

During the last two decades of the 17th century, as a result of the French explorations, guns were sporadically used by both Indians and Europeans in engagements along the Eastern Plains borderlands. Nevertheless, the new weapons did not alter the organization of the military technique patterns, since there were only a small number in circulation, and they were used very infrequently. However, at the turn of the 18th century this situation was markedly altered through the establishment of stable, continuing trade relations between Indians and Europeans in this area.

The French had established the new colony of Louisiana in the lower Mississippi Valley and were expanding outward in every direction. Meanwhile, the settlements in the Illinois country to the north were growing satisfactorily and French traders were rapidly spreading their influence westward from the line of communication between the two colonies, the Mississippi River. Their hearts were set on the distant goal of a lucrative trade in specie with the mining regions of north Mexico. Even in this early period, the English influence, in the form of colonial traders or their Indian middlemen, was present in some force in the southern trans-Mississippi borderlands.

The beaver trade was out of the question in this southern area, since the winters were too mild to produce a marketable pelt. Trade was confined to hides, tallow, some dried or preserved meat, horses, and captives. During the first third of the 18th century the local market for slaves in the Illinois country, Louisiana, and the Canadas was still absorbing a fair number of Indians. However, after this time, the domestic market contracted sharply because the growth of the Illinois country had ceased, while in Louisiana Negro slaves were found superior to Indian and soon formed the vast bulk of the labor supply. Royal decree forbade Louisiana to export Indian slaves to the hungry markets of the West Indies, and what trade there was, was carried on surreptitiously.[1]

The condition in the English colonies was entirely different. Here no restrictive laws interfered with trade, and their continuous, rapid growth required an expanding labor supply. Of the southern colonies, South Carolina was the main one to be engaged in the Indian trade; and in this trade the English always had a competitive advantage over the French, because their wares were both superior and cheaper, and because their markets were readier to absorb Indian goods. Moreover, because of the transportation difficulties, Indian captives were found to be the most profitable commodity which the area west of the Mississippi could exchange with South Carolina. This trade was carried on partly by South Carolinan traders, partly by chains of Indian middlemen involving the Cherokee, Chickasaw, Osage, and marginal Plains Caddoans, and partly on an illegal basis by French "voyageurs" and even the relatives of high government officials.[2] A fair number of these transplanted Indians slaves were absorbed in the domestic market of the southern colonies, especially since the demand for labor had increased sharply with the beginning of large-scale rice cultivation in the coastal lowlands. But the greatest proportion was exported to the West Indies, and sold to obtain money with which to purchase the more desirable Negro slaves on which the growing plantation economy was mainly based.

"Few Guns Period"

Approximately the first two decades of the 18th century may be assigned to the "Few Guns Period," during which time the Gun Frontier advanced sufficiently far west to include the Eastern Plains borderlands Caddoans. It was a transition period, and so included aspects characteristic of both the preceding and following ones. The number of guns present in this period was insufficient to alter the general conduct of, and equipment for, war; but it was sufficient to turn the balance of power against the Apache, although not too tellingly. A contributory factor in this military shift was that, under Apache pressure, the extreme Plainsward Caddoan groups had united with shattered fragments of other tribes to form a new, fairly unified unit known as

[1] Surrey, 1916, pp. 226, 229.

[2] *Ibid.* Also we note, for example, that in 1716 "The Sr. de Ste. Heleine, nephew of S. de Bienville [then governor of Louisiana] was also killed while going secretly to Carolina in order to sell there some slaves. No one gave a reason because they are the savages, allies of the English, who killed him." (Correspondence Générale Louisiane, 1716, Mississippi, p. 23).

the "Wandering Nation." Moreover, these peoples had also completely abandoned horticulture, and had become pure horse nomads. Thus they shared with the Comanche the advantage of elusiveness in relation to their seasonally horticultural Apache foe.

In this "Few Guns Period" trade assumed a very important role among the Caddoans, for despite the fact that it was small and irregular the trickle of guns, ammunition, and other European merchandise nevertheless initiated marked changes in the military, political and economic situation of these tribes. This period also coincided with the closing phase of the Indian slave trade in the Southeast. In their Pregun era the Caddoans had been devastatingly raided for captives by the tribes east of the Mississippi that had formed part of the British trade network centered on South Carolina. Now, with a small supply of guns, they were able to make a decisive change in their relations. They forced the eastern tribes to substitute trading for raiding, made themselves the furthermost extension of the British trade system, and also set up their own system of direct trade with the recently established French Louisiana colony. In this trade Indian captives still played a significant part, but now the Apache to the west were the chief source of supply in place of the Caddoans.[3] For example, when Ulibarri was at El Cuartelejo in 1706, he heard about the war between the Apache and the Pawnee, and learned that the latter had obtained some guns from the French. In addition, the Apache told him that the Pawnee often sold Apache women and children into slavery with the French, just as they themselves sold Pawnee captives in New Mexico.[4]

Toward the close of the period, as the supply of guns mounted, the marginal Caddoans began to expand their hunting grounds westward at the expense of the Apache.[5] The northern groups, to the west of the

[3] A good illustration of the sporadic trade in captives during this period comes from La Harpe's trip to the Caddoan tribes of eastern Oklahoma. In 1719 he visited a compact village on the ". . . southwest branch of the river of Alcansas." (Perhaps this was the Canadian River). This village consisted of a number of tribal fragments, mostly Caddoan. In addition, a large section of the "Wandering Nation" was present at a peace-making ceremony. In return for his gifts they gave, among other things ". . . a little slave of the Cancy [i. e., a Caddoan name for the Apache] nation of eight years, of which they had eaten a finger from each hand, a mark that one was destined to serve one day as food to these cannibals." And a chief told him ". . . that he was sorry to have only one slave to present to me, that if I had arrived a moon sooner he would have given me the seventeen that they had eaten in a public feast." While on "The eleventh there arrived a savage from the Chicachas Nation [i. e., Chickasaw] with merchandise." This Chickasaw was clearly a part of the English trade network extending from South Carolina, and was much disturbed to find a French competitor. (From Lewis, Anna, 1924, pp. 343–44 and p. 347).

[4] Thomas, 1935, p. 19.

[5] *Ibid.*, pp. 4, 20, 31, 131.

Illinois country, apparently had a lead over the rest of the marginal Caddoans in supply of guns. This superiority is suggested by the event which may be considered to close the "Few Guns Period" and to foreshadow the period of ample gun supply immediately following. This event was the total destruction by the Pawnee of a joint Apache and Spanish cavalry expedition, led by Villasur in 1720, at the junction of the North and South Platte Rivers.[6]

The initial surprise which the Pawnee achieved by attacking from ambush at dawn was one factor in the victory, but it was the devastating effect of the volleys from their numerous guns which prevented the invaders from rallying successfully. It is interesting to note that in this battle the Pawnee fought entirely on foot. This may have been due in part to the exigencies of this particular conflict, but it also seems to reflect the need, most strongly felt when only a small proportion of the total force was armed with guns, to get the most efficient performance by fire from afoot. This need tended to reinforce or partially revive the old Pre-horse pattern of infantry warfare. Additional factors were the examples of the Indians to the east, belonging to the Post-gun—Pre-horse tradition, and the French who traded them their guns, all of whom fought on foot.

During this same period, the Plains peoples of the west occasionally obtained guns. Most of these weapons went to the Apache who were holding out against heavy attack by the Ute and Comanche. They acquired some of their firearms from the few exploring French traders, and others from raids on the Pawnee. But the effect was negligible, since they lacked permanent trade contacts to replenish the supply.[7]

Effect of Full Horse and Gun Pattern on Balance of Power

Until about 1727 the Apache continued to defend the northern half of their territory, constantly seeking Spanish military support. But after that date, they fell back south of the Arkansas River under the combined pressure of the Ute and Comanche from the north and west, who had a pure Post-horse—Pre-gun military technique pattern, and the Pawnee groups from the north and east, who had the new, developing Horse *and* Gun pattern. During the seven years from 1720 to 1727 the activities of French trading and exploring parties increased in the northern area, for this was the principal route by which the French sought to penetrate into New Mexico. Although the French traded some guns with the Apache, and even participated in some expeditions against the Ute-Comanche foe,[8] their influence was

[6] Thomas, 1924; also 1935, pp. 37, 171, 174.
[7] *Ibid.*, pp. 36, 74.
[8] *Ibid.*, pp. 256–57.

6

neither great enough nor continuous enough to offset the strong, un-remitting pressures from the Pawnee, Comanche, and Ute.[9] After the Apache abandoned their northern territories, the Comanche occupied the western portion. The French traders made contact with these new clients, at first infrequently as previously, but with increasing intensity as time went on.

The decline of Apache power was now greatly hastened, for surround-ed as they were on the north and east by enemy tribes, and on the south and west by the Spaniards, they were permanently cut off from all sources of guns. The Spaniards in Texas, as elsewhere, obeyed the decrees prohibiting the sale of guns and ammunition to Indians, while the French traders who would gladly have sold such goods, usually had to detour far to the north of the Texas colony which had been ex-pressly founded to block just such French expansion toward north Mexico.[10]

Thus, the Comanche rather than the Apache now benefited from the increasing French efforts to reach that region. The final event which sealed the doom of the Apache was the alliance concluded, about 1740, between the Comanche and the allied Caddoans of eastern Oklahoma and northeast Texas. These latter had acquired a plentiful supply of guns during the preceding twenty years; a way now appeared for the Comanche to do the same. A brisk trade grew up in which the Comanche brought in buffalo hides and meat, Spanish and Apache horses and mules, Apache captives for sale, and Spanish captives for ransom. In exchange they received frequent, plentiful supplies of guns, am-munition, hatchets, knives, pots, and other trade goods.[11] In this new situation the Comanche quickly took over the full Horse *and* Gun mili-tary technique pattern. The Apache were thereby left as the last re-maining carriers of the older Post-horse—Pre-gun pattern, with its use of leather armor for horse and rider and other characteristics, even as they had been the first to develope it.

Now that a sharply declining gradient in the supply of guns—and hence in military power—had been established against the Apache, their enemies to the north and east naturally redoubled their expan-sion into this military near-vacuum, so rich in plunder and good bison hunting grounds. The Apache then begged the Spaniards in Texas for assistance. The result was that the Spaniards made repeated attempts to immobilize the Apache permanently by stationing them in horticultural settlements around the missions where they could theoretically be protected by Spanish forces, as were the Pueblos of New Mexico.[12] However, this policy proved a complete failure, since

[9] *Ibid.*
[10] Bolton, 1914, vol. 1, pp. 58–60, 60–61.
[11] *Ibid.*, pp. 47–48, 103.
[12] Bolton, 1915, pp. 86, 94.

the Apache did not want to give up the nomadic bison-hunting phase of their life, and did not feel safe anchored to the missions, which were easily locatable and ready targets for Comanche raids.[13]

The Spaniards did provide some military assistance by undertaking joint expeditions with the Apache, in order to protect their own Texas colony from the Comanche-Caddoan alliance known as the Norteños. However, following the decisive defeat of the combined Apache-Spanish force under Parilla in 1759 by the Norteños, all such assistance ceased.[14]

The shift in the military balance of power from the Apache to their enemies, and the constantly pressing advance of the latter from the north and east gradually brought about a shift in Spanish-Apache relations. In former times, though the Apache had often raided them for horses, they had also often traded with them; indeed, the more distant Apache groups maintained a rather peaceful trading relation with the Spaniards.[15] By this time, however, all the Apache groups were driven rather close to the Spanish frontiers, and their economic needs had considerably increased. For one thing, the military supremacy of the Comanche and their allies enabled them to make a much greater drain upon the horse herds of the Apache than ever before. They could also attack the Apache encampments successfully, carrying off the metal goods which were so badly needed. Finally, as a result of this hostile pressure, the need of the Apache for guns and ammunition was enormous. At the same time, the Apache were less able than ever to obtain goods to trade with the Spaniards. The enemy's greater strength had cut off the source of supply for the slave trade of the Apache, while his steady encroachment on their remaining bison range made it increasingly difficult to acquire even a surplus of hides and dried meat for trade. Moreover, the Spanish embargo on the sale of guns or ammunition to the Indians still remained. As a result of their greatly increased needs, and their greatly decreased effective economic demand, the Apache trade relation with the Spaniards became increasingly unsatisfactory. Their only alternative was to seize the items they required by force. Hence, by the latter half of the 18th century, when military cooperation and the attempts to settle the Apache around the missions had both been abandoned, the main relation remaining between Spaniards and Apache was a state of war.[16]

[13] *Ibid.*, p. 94.

[14] *Ibid.*, p. 89.

[15] For example, at a Council of War in Santa Fe in 1719, Juan de Archibeque requested that "... war be made against the Ute and Comanche because it is evident that for more than seven or eight years they have come to steal horses and rob herds and run away with the goods in the trade which this kingdom has with the Apaches of El Cuartelejo." (Thomas, 1935, p. 107).

[16] The fact that there was no longer any basis for, or hope of, peace with the Apache is attested by the plans that were made at this time by the Spaniards to

As a result of their weakened position the Apache needed desperately to strengthen themselves with alliances, but they were completely surrounded by tribes whom they had alienated in the period of their own aggressive expansion. To the north and east these tribes had become overwhelmingly powerful through the advance of the Gun Frontier, and they were only too happy to reverse their former roles and prey upon the Apache. However, to the southwest were the "Jumanes,"[17] far away from the Gun Frontier, and hence still weak. This being a matter of mutual advantage, a firm alliance took place between these two groups, formerly bitter enemies.[18]

Under the severe stress of their situation, the easternmost group of the Apache, the Lipan, attempted to open a trade for guns with one of the enemy tribes of east Texas. The Lipan were so successful in this endeavor that the Spaniards at once took note of it as a severe threat.[19] The Spaniards soon put an end to this source of supply, since they were well aware that their control over the hostile tribes depended upon control over trade.[20] At the same time the Apache were being pushed rapidly away from their new trade contact far toward the southwest, and even across the Rio Grande.

This new situation, in which the Apache acquired most of their needed European goods by war, brought about some changes in the nature of the raid against the Spaniards. In the former pattern, raids had usually concentrated on running off horses. As a rule, even small forces were able to accomplish this without much close contact with the enemy, and generally with little loss of life on either side. However, it was now much more often necessary to come to grips with the enemy and kill or defeat him, in order to carry off the guns, ammunition, metal goods, and other items which were on his person or in his dwelling. Naturally, under these circumstances, the war parties tended to be larger and the loss of life much greater, particularly for the Spaniards.

During the first two decades of the 19th century the military organization of the Spanish frontier began to disintegrate as a result of the revolutions and internal strife which preceded the final separation of Mexico from Spain in 1821. After the latter date, the colonial ban

make an alliance with the formerly hostile northern tribes, Comanche and Caddoans, and to undertake a joint campaign for the destruction of all the eastern Apache. (See Bolton, 1914, vol. 1, pp. 110–113).

[17] The "Jumanes" or "Jumano" were apparently a non-Caddoan, non-Athabascan people originally of southwest Texas. They were split and a fragment became intimately associated with the Wichita, while the other section became the "Jumano Apache." (For further discussion of this group, see Bolton, 1911, pp. 66–84).

[18] Dunn, W. E., 1910–11, p. 228.

[19] Bolton, 1914, vol. 2, p. 153.

[20] Bolton, 1915, p. 120.

on trading guns and ammunition with the Indians became entirely ineffective. The situation for the Apache was thereby much improved, for it was possible to raid in one region, frequently north Mexico, and sell part of the loot in another, usually New Mexico. Under these circumstances the Apache were at last able to obtain a fair supply of guns and acquire the full Horse *and* Gun military technique pattern.

However, there is evidence that isolated elements of the older Post-horse—Pre-gun pattern survived well into the middle of the 19th century. For instance, one New Mexico source, dating somewhere between 1812 and 1849, states that "The offensive weapons of the Apache consist of firearms, *lances, bows and arrows.*...Their defensive weapons consist of *rawhide armor and shield*...[21] Again, the Pima have preserved a memory of one Apache raid in the mid-19th century. The Pima had been surprised at their annual saguaro cactus drunk, but

... they overtook the party of Apaches and killed five of them. On examining the dead Apaches it was found that their bodies were protected with *rawhide armor*; then the Pimas understood why their arrows had glanced off or jumped back.[22]

[21] Carroll and Haggard, 1942, p. 200. Italics FRS.
[22] Russell, 1903, p. 78. Italics FRS.

CHAPTER EIGHT

DISCUSSION

To be most meaningful the present study of Plains military technique patterns must be viewed within the broader framework of Plains culture change. The traditional culture area approach was perhaps most explicitly elaborated for the Plains by Wissler.[1] However, a funtional-historical approach finds the original form of this schema far too static. It required a marked geographic stability of the tribes as a necessary condition for the fixed culture center with its radiating influences. Yet time perspective reveals this as an area of especially vast and rapid tribal expansions, contractions and migrations. Hence, a progressive revision of this traditional view of the Plains area has been under way for some time. Both Strong[2] and Kroeber[3] have criticized the demonstrable lack of historical depth in the traditional concept. Strong's work has shown that prior to the influences of white contact the Plains area was clearly dominated by sedentary horticultural groups rather than by nomadic hunters. Kroeber has pointed out that this fact means that during the pre-contact phase the Plains had no existence as a separate culture area, since its dominant groups were culturally subordinated to the intense influences from the great southeastern and northeastern horticultural centers.[4]

By combining Kroeber's[5] dynamic view of culture centers with the specific picture of historical depth formulated in this work, it is possible to provide a more meaningful framework for the interpretation of culture problems in the Plains. Thus, prior to 1600, we may see the Plains natural area as lacking a culture center and being split into eastern sedentary horticultural and western pedestrian, nomadic hunting sub-areas. The eastern territory formed the western periphery of the great eastern North American horticultural region, and was, as Kroeber notes,[6] doubly dependent upon the northeastern and southeastern centers of this area. The archaeological record indicates the early development and continuous existence of these two mutually influenced culture centers in the horticultural east.[7] Thus, down through

---

[1] See Wissler, 1914, 1915a, 1926.
[2] Strong, 1935 and 1936.
[3] Kroeber, 1947.
[4] *Ibid.*, p. 77.
[5] *Ibid.*, especially Chapter XV, "Cultural Intensity and Climax," pp. 222–228.
[6] *Ibid.*, p. 77.
[7] The long persistence of these two main centers is an inference of the author,

time, the western extension of the horticultural area onto the Plains was dominated by whichever one of the two eastern culture centers happened to be the most active at that particular period. For example, at an early period there is definite evidence for the extension of an attenuated Hopewellian culture influence as far west as eastern and central Kansas.[8] Moreover, in the later period, the Arikara, Pawnee, and Wichita clearly represent an extension north and west of a south-eastern culture influence. At the same time, the western frontier of this horticultural sphere of influence fluctuated east and west almost from one border of the Plains natural area to the other, apparently in conjunction with the shifts in climate.[9]

The pre-1600 hunting cultures of the Western Plains are not well known, but there seems to be little to distinguish them from the hunting and gathering cultures west and north of the Plains, except the use of dog transport with the small travois, the small leather tipi, and a dependence on the bison as the staple food. These cultures were too under-developed and the culture elements too uniformly diffused to permit one to speak of anything resembling a culture center. This is the old Pre-horse Plains culture which Wissler[10] claimed was merely intensified by the horse. However, he was unable to give it any more distinctive content than that just mentioned.

After 1600 the old aboriginal culture center in the Southwest was altered by the addition of Spanish culture. The resulting new center of cultural influences had a far greater effect on the adjacent Plains area than the preceding aboriginal Puebloan culture center. The adoption of the horse by the nomad hunters, in this case the eastern Apache, suddenly produced a highly active culture center on the Plains, itself, where none had existed before. In this rapid ferment of culture growth actual basic inventions[11] were absent or rare, as is usually the case, but there were many improving inventions,[12] borrowings, re-combinations of previously existing elements, and shifts in cultural emphasis. Indeed, a new culture was produced which radiated its influence and expanded throughout most of the Plains. It was this culture center which developed that solid foundation of equipment, techniques, and activities upon which the late period erected the characteristic ceremonial, organizational, and decorative superstructure of the so-called "Typical" Plains culture. This study has traced the development

partly from the summary of the archaeological evidence for the Eastern area in Martin, Quimby, and Collier, 1947. See especially pp. 259–88 for the "Ohio Area", and pp. 344–368 for the "Middle Southern Area."

[8] Wedel, 1938, pp. 99–106; 1940, pp. 291–352; 1943.

[9] Wedel, 1941.

[10] Wissler, 1914.

[11] Linton, 1936, pp. 316–320.

[12] *Ibid.*

of the Post-horse—Pre-gun military technique pattern in this Southwestern Plains culture center and has described its diffusion outward over most of the Plains.

In some respects this new culture was merely imitative, but originality is clearly seen at many points. For example, the horse was borrowed and the riding equipment of the Spaniards was rather fully reproduced, as Wissler[13] has said. However, the horse was mounted from the right-hand side, since the use of the sword was not adopted.[14] The sword blade was changed in function by being used to tip the lance. We have also pointed out that the leather armor of the Post-horse—Pre-gun military technique pattern represented a creative fusion of native and Spanish leather armor traditions.[15]

It is true that, in the case of one of the uses of the horse, that in which the horse was substituted for the dog in pulling the travois, this use was directly modeled on the aboriginal transport pattern. However, the acquisition of a larger draft animal permitted an increased size for both travois and tipi, since the same poles were used for both. In contrast, the perfection of the technique of the mounted archer was neither an imitation of the Spaniards,[16] nor the mere substitution of a new element in an aboriginal pattern. It involved a new integration of native and borrowed elements. Moreover, this development involved a whole new complex of group activities. The mounted archer was used in war, and he was also, as a bison hunter, the primary agent in obtaining food. It was inevitable that new techniques of social coordination should develope, suited to the large-scale, mounted bison hunt. Thus, it was necessary, by various means, to control the hunting activities of the individual in order to prevent a bison herd from being stampeded away from a camp, and to enable all of the hunters to attack the herd in concert. It was likewise inevitable that this improved means of food-getting would provide an economic basis allowing the formation of large camps.

Interestingly enough, under the particular conditions then existing, the development of the full horse complex, instead of inhibiting horticulture, actually greatly promoted it. So long as the Post-horse—Pre-gun military technique pattern was the exclusive possession of a single people whose subdivisions were at peace with one another (such as was the case with the Plains Apache), it gave them a great military advantage over their enemies, and hence, a considerable security.

---

[13] Wissler, 1915b.

[14] See this monograph, Chap. II, pp. 26–27.

[15] See this monograph, Chap. II, pp. 14–18, especially p. 17–18.

[16] As our description of Spanish military equipment (given on pp. 14–15) indicates, the mounted archer was distinctly absent. The only occurrence of archery was in the form of the crossbow used by infantrymen.

Under conditions of military security, the nomadic, bison-hunting life did not prove incompatible with the sedentary horticultural life. Indeed, both of them were combined in one annual cycle which exploited the Plains environment to the fullest. However, once military security was lacking, the horticultural sedentary phase proved a weak point, and was either eliminated from the culture, or remained as a continual drain on the vitality of the group. Thus, the Apache flourished under their dual economic cycle until the source of their military supremacy and security, the Post-horse—Pre-gun military technique pattern, was effectively copied and implemented by the Comanche and the composite Caddoan groups, the "Wandering Nation." This equalization of military potential made the horticultural phase of Apache life a military liability, and other tribes, such as the Comanche, had no desire to adopt it. In the later 19th century too, eastern Plains tribes such as the Pawnee, lacking special military advantages, found their horticultural phase a great handicap.[17]

Thus, these new patterns of warfare, subsistence, and transportation were elaborated in the recently formed Southwestern Plains culture center in the mid-17th century, and they spread rapidly north and east over nearly the whole Plains. This cultural diffusion began with the explosive expansion of the Apache and the Shoshoneans, but later spread beyond them to the other tribes. By about 1740, the Apache, northern Shoshoneans, and Comanche, all of whom had benefited early from the new culture center, occupied between them practically all of the High Plains, and hence, nearly half of the total Plains natural area. But by this time the creativity of the Southwestern Plains culture center had declined. Its cultural developments diffused beyond it to other regions where they were equally intensively employed, and it ceased to be a center.

In the third quarter of the 18th century, a second culture center arose in the Plains. This approximated the region around the Black Hills and extended from there to the village tribe sites on the Upper Missouri. As a result of diffusion and the migration of tribes, three influences met at this region. The first and most fundamental was the influence from the Southwestern Plains center, which provided the pattern that was basic to the mounted, nomadic Plains life. The second was derived from the sedentary horticultural village tribes along the upper Missouri, although it had originated at an earlier period with the old southeastern and northeastern centers of the eastern horticultural area. The third was from the contemporary western section of the Northeastern Woodlands, and it was carried principally by the Sioux.

The interaction of these three influences in this general area fostered a phase of cultural creativity that was based upon the cultural influence

[17] See Lesser, 1933; Strong, 1935.

from the Southwestern Plains center, and that flowered into the super-structure of elements and complexes which distinguished Wissler's "most characteristic" Plains tribes of the late 19th century. Indeed, it seems highly probable that both the Sun Dance[18] and the typical Men's Societies were developed here.[19] Moreover, the influence of this Northern Plains center spread rapidly and widely throughout most of the Plains. By the mid-19th century this center appears to have shifted to the west and south of the Black Hills, as a consequence of the migration of the most culturally dynamic tribes, and at the same time, to have begun to fade and disintegrate, as the flow of new cultural creations declined, and as the original developments were widely diffused and the original participating tribes, such as the Crow, Kiowa, Cheyenne, Arapaho and the westernmost Dakota, were drawn off by migration to the west and south.

The development and spread of the specific military technique patterns occurred as an integral part of this general picture of Plains culture change. In the early post-contact period the introduction of the gun and the horse from opposite borders of the Plains area led to the development of two different patterns of military technique: the Post-horse—Pre-gun pattern and the Post-gun—Pre-horse pattern.

The Post-horse—Pre-gun pattern developed in the Southwestern Plains, and consisted of a functionally related complex of material and non-material elements. The warrior fought on horseback using the short bow, lance, and war club; he was protected by a leather shield and leather armor. His horse was also protected by leather armor and equipped with a bridle, bit, and high-pommeled, high-cantled saddle with stirrups. In addition, the Post-horse—Pre-gun pattern included the tactical concept of the large-scale, pitched battle between two lines of cavalry.

The Post-gun—Pre-horse pattern appeared in the Northern Plains. However, in the eastern section of this area it emerged as a slight modification of the Eastern Woodlands pattern. The warrior was on foot and consistently armed with a gun. As secondary equipment he might carry a hatchet or a knife. Large formations were employed when necessary, and when this was the case, they were relatively compact; but they were deployed irregularly and without being held in line.

In the western section of the Northern Plains area the Post-gun—Pre-horse pattern took a somewhat different form. In its early phase, it was largely blocked from expansion onto the Plains by the local trade situation which seriously interfered with the flow of guns from the forest area. At a later period, after a good supply of guns had been made available to the Plains, a fusion took place between the Post-

[18] Spier, 1921, p. 451.
[19] Wissler, 1911.

horse—Pre-gun pattern and the Post-gun—Pre-horse pattern. On the Northwestern Plains, the resultant Horse *and* Gun pattern exhibited two types of battle formation: the cavalry battle, characteristic of the Post-horse—Pre-gun pattern, and the battle of infantry lines. This latter form was probably developed by the interaction of two influences: the use of the gun on foot from the Post-gun—Pre-horse pattern and the formation of the warriors into two regular opposing lines, either directly or indirectly, from the old Pre-horse—Pre-gun pattern of the Northwestern Plains.

The Post-horse—Pre-gun pattern developed earlier and spread widely over the Plains. It was first diffused over the Southern Plains by the expansion of the Apache, its originators. The Caddoans of the eastern margin of the Southern Plains adopted it in self-defense. Next it spread to the Shoshoneans in the north, who then expanded explosively over much of the Northern Plains.

The Post-gun—Pre-horse pattern became established on the Northern Plains at a somewhat later date. In the early 18th century the two patterns met along the upper Missouri River, in the Northeastern Plains, and along the Plains-Forest margin in the Northwestern Plains. Here, a fusion of the two, the Horse *and* Gun military technique pattern was evolved, and it spread west and south with the advancing Gun Frontier to cover the whole Plains. This last pattern is the one recorded by the 19th century sources as representing the "Typical" Plains culture.

This Horse *and* Gun pattern retained much from the Post-horse—Pre-gun pattern, partly in the form of second choice alternatives. Thus, while the gun was as widely used as the particular trade situation permitted, the bow persisted among that fraction of warriors who could not acquire firearms. Battle-field dominance of the gun with its far greater penetrative power rendered leather armor obsolete. Yet the leather shield remained. It was relatively easy to make. Light and handy, it was a locus of protective magic and a fairly effective defense against archery.

The gun also caused a great diminution in the use of the lance. This, together with the abandonment of the heavy, cumbersome body armor, led to a shift in the riding equipment. Bridle and stirrups remained, but the saddle was shifted from the high-pommeled, high-cantled type that gave a more secure seat to the simple leather pad type. Such a saddle left the warrior free to substitute mounted acrobatics, as a technique of defense, for leather armor. Tactical concepts for the organization of large-scale cavalry actions persisted.

The existence of opposing gradients in the concentration of horses and guns, running from the south and west to the north and east, was the fundamental factor which determined the course of development of the various military technique patterns. Thus, the advance of the northern and eastern margin of the horse gradient, the Horse Frontier, practically coincided with the advance of the Post-horse—Pre-gun pattern. At a later date, when the Gun Frontier, moving in the opposite direction, overlapped the Horse Frontier, the progress of the former marked the advance of the Horse *and* Gun military technique pattern.

The location of a given society on one side or the other of one of these frontiers and its position on either the horse or gun gradient had a great effect on its survival potential. Thus, both the Apache in the south and the Shoshoneans in the north were originally located on and behind the Horse Frontier. These tribes took advantage of their Post-horse—Pre-gun military technique pattern to expand widely with that frontier. Later, they dropped well behind the Horse Frontier, but they maintained their conquests, since they were still higher on the horse gradient than other tribes. However, because the Apache and the Shoshoneans, with the single exception of the Comanche, were unable to cross into the region behind the advancing Gun Frontier, they were eventually driven almost completely out of the Plains by the tribes from the north and east that had acquired the Horse *and* Gun pattern.

Moreover, the absolute dependence of these post-contact military technique patterns upon the flow of horses and guns into the Great Plains led to a marked interdependence between war and trade. Horses could be acquired by two methods: raiding and trading. In the case of guns and ammunition raiding was relatively unsatisfactory, and the only steady, dependable source was through trade. Thus trade became of immense importance and all the factors which influenced its intensity had an effect on war because of this linkage.

There were two major phases in the history of trade into the Plains area. The first, which occurred prior to the 19th century, was characterized by a low intensity and a continual shortage of mediums of exchange on the part of the Indians. In this phase a relatively active trade generally accelerated war against adjacent groups, especially those having a less favorable trade situation. In turn, successful warfare stimulated trade by a partial alleviation of the exchange shortage. Lack of success in war produced the opposite effect.

However, after the beginning of the 19th century the massive expansion of the fur trade throughout the Plains produced a period of intense trade. The great new market for the hides of Plains animals and for horses converted a condition of Indian exchange shortage into one of relative abundance. In this phase the connection between trade and war was qualitatively lessened by the development of an abundant source of exchange dependent upon hunting rather than war. Thus, the trade in hides now made it far more feasible than before to buy the amount of equipment that was necessary for tribal defense. At the same time it made plunder far less important in maintaining the required trade minimum. However, any resultant tendency for a decrease in warfare was generally counteracted by another aspect of the situation. The new economy of abundance provided the individual with an increased opportunity and incentive for the acquisition of prestige by achieving a position of special advantage in the flow of wealth. Horse raiding provided one of the greatest and quickest returns, and considerable energy was therefore devoted to it.[20]

In conclusion, we may note that this study of Plains military technique patterns reveals certain inadequacies in the culture pattern concept, both as it has been applied in general and in the Plains area in particular.[21] In brief, the culture pattern approach has concentrated on an interesting, but definitely limited, aspect of culture: namely, the part of any given culture that tends to form a system which is not only self-contained within this culture, but which is also self-determining with respect to its next phase of development. Thus, in "The Vision in Plains Culture,"[22] Benedict chose to investigate the religious aspect of various Plains cultures. Her analysis indicated that, although certain basic religious traits were common to a number of cultures, in each culture that she investigated these traits had been formed into a structure, or "pattern," which was entirely different from that of other cultures. Likewise, she found that external factors exerted only a very indirect effect on such systems or "patterns"—that it was the existing configuration of culture elements which mainly determined whether new culture elements, available through contacts with other cultures, would be rejected or accepted, and, if the latter, how they would be integrated into the final cultural form.

However, a focus on military technique patterns, as in the present study, throws into sharp relief one part of culture which clearly does not fit the culture pattern assumptions. There are undoubtedly other segments of culture which could also be used to illustrate this. In the case of military technique patterns in the Plains area the evidence cited in the body of this monograph indicates that, at any given time, each of the three patterns (i. e., Post-horse—Pre-gun, Post-gun—Pre-horse, and Horse *and* Gun) was fundamentally the same in both content and organization from culture to culture throughout its area of distribution. This uniformity is a good indication that the military technique pattern of a given culture formed part of a system which involved the corresponding parts of a number of different cultures.

The basis for this situation was three-fold. In the first place, war, by

[20] For discussions of trade, war, social structure, and social character in this late period see: Mishkin, 1940; Lewis, Oscar, 1942; Goldfrank, 1943; Jablow, 1951.
[21] Good examples of this approach are Benedict, 1922 and 1934.
[22] Benedict, 1922.

its very nature, involves an interaction between different societies. In a homogeneous culture area which has a long history undisturbed by significant influences or migrations from the outside, the largest social units will tend to have nearly identical cultures. Thus, the largest cultural unit will be coterminous with the culture area, itself, and will contain many of the largest social units. Under these circumstances war among the societies of the area does not mean an interaction between different cultures. However, the Plains in the period covered by this study was a culture area of completely opposite characteristics. It was newly formed out of a medley of tribes, some original inhabitants of the natural area and many others, immigrants from the diverse surrounding culture areas. Thus, in the Plains the largest social units tended to be coterminous with the largest cultural units, and war implied an interaction between different cultures in at least their military aspects.

In the second place, war is a struggle and competition between societies for victory, in one sense or another, and for survival. This produces a condition more than superficially analogous to that of natural selection in the biological world. Individual variation is produced by diffusion as well as local invention and development. The struggle for sheer survival, as well as varying degrees of prosperity, is provided by war among a number of societies, each with its own culture. In this situation a new military technique pattern will compete with the previously existing pattern of the area, and the more efficient will spread at the expense of the less efficient. Thus, the Horse *and* Gun pattern gradually spread south and west over the Great Plains at the expense of the Post-horse—Pre-gun pattern.

Under these conditions a given society with a particular culture will be powerfully influenced from outside the culture by a great incentive, and by a great pressure to adopt the more efficient military technique pattern. If, for any reason, due either to circumstances external to the particular society and culture or to the internal organizing influence of other parts of the culture on the military technique patterns, it is not possible to respond to the externally generated forces by a substitution of the new and more efficient pattern for the original pattern, the society with its particular culture will either be destroyed or forced into a territorial retreat. This process is vividly illustrated in the case of the Northern Plains Shoshoneans and the Southern Plains Apache who were unable to shift from the Post-horse—Pre-gun pattern to the Horse *and* Gun pattern until very late, and who consequently were nearly completely driven out of the Plains area.

In the third place, the implementation of any of the military technique patterns in the Plains, except for that of the Pre-horse—Pre-gun period, was only possible through trading and raiding relations.

Thus, a particular social unit having a particular culture could only obtain the necessary horses, guns, powder, and other equipment by means of relations with other societies, and these mainly had different cultures.

It is evident, then, that the military technique pattern of any one culture was largely formed in response to external influences from other cultures in the spheres of war and trade. The strength of these external influences is illustrated in this study by the speed with which all cultures that came in contact with a superior military technique pattern adopted that pattern, unless clearly prevented from doing so by temporarily insurmountable, external political or trade barriers. The existence of a linkage between the military technique pattern of a given culture and those other aspects of the culture, such as religion, which formed self-contained systems within the culture is unquestioned. But the strength of that linkage, in terms of its influence on the form of the military technique pattern of the culture, appears minimal when viewed in relation to the strength of the influences coming from outside cultures. Hence, the culture pattern approach is an ineffective tool for the investigation of those aspects of a given culture which, like the military technique pattern, actually have their most potent connections with the similar aspects of a number of other cultures, thus forming a multi-cultural system.

A complete and comprehensive picture of any one culture will be best secured by first distinguishing, in each individual case, between those aspects of the culture, which are integrated into systems predominantly internal to the culture, and those aspects, which are predominantly linked to aspects of other cultures, thus forming multi-cultural systems. The next step is to investigate these two phases of culture by the method most appropriate to each of them. The final stage is to show the functional interrelation and development of all aspects of the culture in time depth.

The use of the Flintlock Muzzle-Loader on Horseback

The feasibility of using the flintlock muzzle-loader on horseback is frequently questioned. I shall, therefore, present briefly some relevant data on this point.

There were several varieties of flintlock muzzle-loaders. Those ordinarily used by footmen were very long and heavy. Others, however, were short and light; and it was the latter type that was used, not only by the mounted Plains Indians, but also by European cavalry.

After the initial period of trade contact, the North American tribes always developed very specific demands as to the nature of the various types of goods for which they traded. American traders entering a region formerly served by British traders usually found that American-made cloth did not come up to Indian standards, and they were generally forced to import the specified types and colors of cloth from the superior English mills.

That the same situation obtained with respect to guns and Indian selectivity is graphically illustrated from correspondence of the American Fur Company. A requisition to the company from its St. Louis agent in 1832 notes

The North West Guns are one of the articles most important in our business, and our traders in general complain of those of this year, especially in the posts of the Upper Missouri, where they make the most use of them. The stocks are a little too heavy, and not crooked enough, — but the worst of it is that every stock is made of two pieces joined at the breech and this the Indians cannot endure. When the Stock is new and varnished, you hardly discover this imperfection, but when they have been used, or exposed to the wet, it has an ugly effect, and very often the Indians bring them back to be exchanged for better, or those who have them on credit will not pay for them.[1]

Furthermore, we see this selectivity operating as a major factor forcing the American Fur Company to buy abroad rather than from domestic factories:

Preference in the trade for North West guns of English make is stressed in several letters from the Fur Company to James Henry, who succeeded his father J. Joseph Henry [owner and operator of the Boulton Gun Works, near Nazareth, Pennsylvania] in 1836; "We have already sent our requisitions to England for probably all we shall require .... We cannot hold out any encouragement for North West guns. Our people will not take any but the English." At this time

[1] Parsons, 1952, p . 183.

the Company was ordering direct from abroad, through Lacy & Reynolds of London and William Chance Son & Co. of Birmingham.[2]

Now, in order to establish the characteristics of the North West Gun, we must assemble sets of partial information from several sources. One tells us that an order of 580 North West guns consisted of "flint-lock smoothbores, walnut or maple stocked with square butts, and ordered usually according to length of barrel, from 2 feet 6 inches to 4 feet."[3] The average length of the portion of the stock extending from the butt of the barrel to the butt of the gun is approximately 15″. By adding this factor to the lengths of barrels just quoted we find that the overall lengths of this particular lot of North West guns ranged from $3^3/_4{}'$ to $5^1/_4{}'$. Thus, in regard to length, the shorter of these guns were well suited to mounted use, while the longer ones, say anything much over 4′, were only useful on foot. The American Fur Company also offered rifles for sale to the Indians, and in this category of merchandise the U. S. product was clearly superior. Hence,

... with regard to rifles, the Fur Company steadfastly gave its patronage to the Pennsylvania gunsmiths, even when procuring the "English" pattern. An order of December 23, 1830 is directed to four Lancaster makers .... Speci-fications were for both single and double-trigger weapons, "3 feet 6–$^1/_2$ to 3 feet 8 inches in the Barrel, to carry a ball 32 to 40 to the pound .... Each gun when complete to weigh about 10 lb...."[4]

Since the overall length of this weapon was approximately $4^3/_4{}'$ to 5′, it would be most unwieldy for mounted use. Likewise the weight was excessive, not to mention the fact that the rifling made it an ab-solute necessity before each shot to use the ramrod with considerable vigor in order to force the lead ball down against the charge. Thus, in spite of the greater range and accuracy of the rifle, the mounted tribes of the Great Plains continued to buy the short variety of the North West gun, while the tribes of the Woodlands quickly shifted from the long, smoothbore musket to the long rifle. This is clearly the explanation for the statement that "The North West Guns are one of the articles most important in our business... especially in the posts of the Upper Missouri, where they make the most use of them."[5]

Our next source of information comes from the description of one of the rare museum specimens. This North West gun, property of the Chicago Historical Society, dates from the late 18th century. The caliber is approximately .55, overall length 43″, full length stock 39″, barrel length 27″, wooden ramrod, total weight $5^3/_4$ lbs., and it was made by

[2] *Ibid.*, p. 183–84.
[3] *Ibid.*, p. 183.
[4] *Ibid.*, p. 185–86.
[5] *Ibid.*, p. 183.

W. Chance & Son of London.[6] This gun is an excellent example of the type of musket sought by the Plains horseman. Its length of about $3^1/_2'$ is quite handy, and its very light weight made it possible to hold and shoot using only the right arm. Thus, the left arm was free to manage the leather shield and the reins. The extreme lightness of this gun is most clearly realized when we note that the standard infantry musket was almost twice as heavy. A good example of the typical infantry weapon is given by the French Smoothbore Musket Model 1763 (Charleville) which was closely copied by U.S. armories until this type of gun went out of existence shortly after the middle of the 19th century: "Caliber .69, smooth-bore, taking a 16 gauge, one ounce ball. Total length $59-^7/_8$ inches, weight with bayonet $9-^3/_4$ to $10-^1/_2$ pounds.... The Stock is ... 57 inches long.... The Barrel is $44-^3/_4$ inches long..."[7] It is clear that such a weapon as this, about 5 feet in length and 10 pounds in weight, is most unsuited for mounted use.

A final source of information on the "North West" type gun comes from U.S. government records. In the period following the Revolutionary War, when it was United States policy to expand west and north into the territory formerly dominated by Britain, the government sponsored and guided the Indian trade. In order to capture this trade the Americans had to compete with British traders. Under these conditions Indian selectivity forced them to provide the desired English type trade guns. In an attempt to achieve independence from English factories the U.S. government assigned the manufacture of a suitable gun to one of its own armories, and the characteristics of this weapon thus must closely reflect those of one type of the English "North West Gun".

> The first carbine to be made at our national armories was in reality designed not as a martial weapon [i. e., not for use by the United States Army], but as a light-weight, half-ounce caliber, smooth bore, wood ramrod, pinned stock arm, made for the Indian Department. Meant for use of Indians friendly to the nation; .... U. S. Flintlock Carbine Model 1807. Caliber .54, smoothbore, taking a ball 32 to the pound. Total length $48-^1/_2$ inches. Weight about 5 pounds ... full length stock ... $45-^3/_4$ inches long ... barrel ... $33^3/_4$ inches long.... These arms, 1,200 of which were authorized in 1807 for manufacture by the Secretary of War, Henry Dearborn, ... went into production the same year, and a total of 1,202 were recorded to have been completed at the Springfield Armory in 1809–1810.[8]

Such a weapon was light enough and short enough to be handled with relative ease on horseback.

Moreover, the use of the light, flintlock muzzle-loader by the Plains

---

[6] With the kind permission of Mr. Wm. S. Willis this information has been extracted from two personal communications of Sept. 25 and Dec. 3, 1952 received by him from H. Maxson Holloway, Curator, Chicago Historical Society.

[7] Gluckman, 1948, pp. 56–57.

[8] *Ibid.*, pp. 348–49.

Indian is graphically described by a U. S. Army Officer who had spent thirty-three years on the Plains. In speaking of the first half of the nineteenth century before the Indians were equipped with the breech-loading rifle and metal cartridges he states that

... many [of the mounted Indians] were armed with guns of the most nonde-script character, old Tower muskets, and smooth-bores of every antique pattern. Powder and lead were easily obtained from the traders. The former was carried in a horn, the latter was cut into pieces, which were roughly hammered into spherical form. These bullets were purposely made so much smaller than the bore of the gun as to run down when dropped into the muzzle. When going into a fight, the Indian filled his mouth with bullets. After firing he reloaded in full career, by turning up the powder-horn, pouring into his gun an unknown quantity of powder, and then spitting a bullet into the muzzle.[9]

Cavalry played only a small part in the Revolutionary War. Indeed, it did not develop as a significant branch of the United States Army until American frontier expansion had carried army activity out of the eastern forested area onto the western prairies and plains. It then became necessary to manufacture a firearm adapted for mounted use. Hence, we note the characteristics of the following weapons:

U.S. Flintlock Musketoon Model 1839. Caliber .69, smoothbore, taking an ounce ball. Total length 41 inches. Weight about 7 pounds, 3 ounces.[10]

Musketoons, short barreled arms, the length of a carbine, but full stocked, were authorized for the Artillery, Cavalry, and for Sappers in 1847.[11]

U.S. Artillery Musketoon Model 1847. Caliber .69, smoothbore. Total length 41 inches. Weight about six pounds 6 ounces.... The black walnut full stock was 38-$\frac{1}{4}$ inches long .... The barrel was 26 inches long .... The barrel was held to the forestock by two (iron) bands .....[12]

U.S. Cavalry Musketoon Model 1847. This arm is essentially identical with the artillery musketoon Model 1847, described above, except that the furniture was brass, the bayonet stud was omitted, a sling ring was added. The swivel type, button end ramrod was attached to a stud fixed under the barrel...[13]

U.S. Cavalry Musketoon Model 1851. The swivel type method of ramrod attachment of the Model 1847 cavalry Musketoon having been found unhandy and difficult to manage for loading on horseback, in 1851, Model 1847 cavalry Musketoons were modified by attaching the ramrod to the barrel by a sleeve chain. The barrels of some were rifled...[14]

The advance of the frontier out of the Woodland onto the Plains similarly forced a change in the "Kentucky" long rifle, the standard equipment of the frontiersmen, to adapt it for use on horseback. Thus,

The "plains rifle" that came to be used by Carson and his contemporaries was quite dissimilar to the one used in the day Kit made his first trip to Santa Fe.

[9] Dodge, 1882, p. 450.
[10] Gluckman, 1948, p. 350.
[11] *Ibid.*, p. 352.
[12] *Ibid.*, p. 351–352.
[13] *Ibid.*, p. 353.
[14] *Ibid.*, p. 354.

That rifle was the Pennsylvania-made one which, as it was carried westward, became commonly known as a "Kentucky" rifle. It was still the type of rifle that had been used by the frontiersmen in their taming of the territory east of the Mississippi; a rifle adapted to the use of men afoot in a heavily wooded country. This lineal descendant of the old German jaeger rifle was, in its turn, to undergo changes that would render it more suitable for use by horsemen of the Plains.

Carson's early days in the West were the latter ones of the long-barreled, full-stocked flintlock; for as economic conditions forced the mountain trappers into Plains service the cumbersomeness of their long rifles became increasingly apparent. Those of the Plains Indians who already possessed firearms were showing a marked preference for guns with shorter barrels and bigger bores. Even their Northwest Company fusils — smoothbore, flintlock trade guns — lent themselves better to the needs of horsemen.... To Jacob Hawkins, a Saint Louis gunsmith, goes much credit for materializing the experience-bred demands of the riflemen who rode in from the West. He lightened their rifles by cutting a good six inches or more from the barrel; this, in turn, usually called for a half-stock.... "Pea rifle" calibers were definitely of the past, for the Plains rifles were all of calibers corresponding to the larger long rifle bores — .38 to .55. The barrels averaged 34 inches in length.[15]

After the reconquest of New Mexico at the end of the 17th century the Spanish military forces were composed of cavalry exclusively. A letter, dated 1719 and written by the local commander in New Mexico asking for more modern guns to meet the threat of a French invasion from the east, shows us what the prevailing equipment was like. Speaking of the local army units, he says,

> Because up to now these companies may have been considered sufficient for the Indians, their discipline and arms makes them incapable of resisting trained troops because their firelocks which they commonly use are about five spans long [1 span being 9 inches] and of such small caliber that they serve only for defense against arrows and not for firelocks and other guns of range, which must be considered with regard to any enemies other than Indians.[16]

From this we gather that the guns of the local Spanish cavalry were about 3¾ feet in length, which is a good length for a horseman. Also, when he speaks of them as being a "defense against arrows," he clearly means that they were a superior weapon to the bow. This was undoubtedly due to their greater penetrative power, because the same source infers elsewhere[17] that their present guns do not outrange the bow.

Turning to Europe, we shall note only a few typical selections illustrating the use of the muzzle-loading flintlock by cavalry. The first citation is from the work of an English professional soldier, written sometime in the 1580's. Regarding the use of firearms (at this period often matchlock rather than flintlock) by horsemen, he notes that

---

[15] Lenz, 1944, pp. 136–37.
[16] Thomas, 1935, p. 153
[17] *Ibid.*, p. 146.

Although the musket be a weapon of greater force then the Harquebuze is of, yet generally both on horseback and on foote, a Harquebuze dooth serve for both.[18]

Also, from his professional knowledge of the performance of military equipment, he gives his opinion

...touching the arming of light horsemen, as Hargolets, Petronels, and Pistolliers:.... Then a good sword and a dagger: for weapons, either a Harquebuze with a snaphance, or a Speare and one Pistoll, or else three Pistols two in cases and one at his girdle, or at the hinder part of his saddle: I do account the Harquebuze and the Petronels all as one, and these should be for these kindes of Light horsemen.[19]

The next citation gives a picture of cavalry in late 17th century England after the period of the Civil War:

There were and are to be taken notice of five several kinds of men at arms for the Horse service
        [Lanceirs
        [Cuirasiers
        [Arquebuziers...
        [Carabiniers
        [Dragoniers
3. Arquebuziers, who are very serviceable and are to be armed defensive with a good Buff coat, and to have a back, breast, and pot Pistoll proofe: and for his offensive armes, he is to have a good Harquebuz, hanging on a Belt, with a swivel, and serviceable Pistols, as is set forth in the Horse service by act of Parliament for the service of the Militia, but rather somewhat larger, and a good cutting sword.... 4. Carabiniers are to be armed as the Harquebuziers, their Horses may be somwhat lesser, but for the offensive arms instead of the Harquebuz, a good Carabine, hanging on a belt with a swivel, by the ring of the Carabine; but for Pistols and Swords, they must be according to the act of Parliament for the arming of a Militia Trooper, ... The service of them in execution is not to be disputed; the Experienced Souldier can testifie enough of the singular benefit they are of in service; .... 5. The Dragonier. Dragoones are but Foot, (to be) on horseback and are so mounted for the expedition of their march...[20]

The Exercising of a Troop, as armed with a Carabine, and Pistol. The Horse being in a body to exercise, and to make the Souldier more able to handle his armes, when he shall be called forth to fight; the words of Command shall follow.... The words of Command for the Carabine. [The troop being in the saddle]. All the Carabines being dropt (let fall) and hanging by their Swivells; The Postures are as followeth. Silence being commanded. 1. Handle your Carabine. 2. Mount your Carabine, placing your butt end upon your Thigh. 3. Rest your Carabine in your bridle hand. 4. Bend your cock, to half bent. 5. Guard (or secure) your cock. 6. Prime your Pan. 7. Shut your pan, (or fix your hammer). 8. Sink your Carabine on your left side. 9. Gage your flask. 10. Lade your Carabine. 11. Draw forth your scouring stick (or Rammer). 12. Shorten your Rammer. 13. Lade with Bullet and Ramm home. 14. With-draw your Rammer, (or scouring stick). 15. Return your scouring stick. 16. Recover and rest your Carabine in your bridlehand.

[18] Barwick, 1580–90, p. 10.
[19] *Ibid.*, p. 22.
[20] Venn, 1672, pp. 7–8.

17. Fix your Hammer, (or Steel). 18. Free your Cock. 19. Present your Carabine. In presenting of the Carabine, he must rest it upon his bridle arm, placing the butt end to the right side near the shoulder; or at length with his right hand. 20. Give fire. Note; That the Carabine is to be fired about twelve foot distance, and to be levelled at the knees of your Enemies Horse, because that by the strength of the Powder and motion of the Horse your shot may be at Random. 21. Drop (or let fall) your Carabine. These postures may serve for the Harquebuz; but observe, when at any time you make your approaches towards an Enemy, your Carabine is to be mounted, with the butt end on your thigh, with your hand above the lock; and so when you march through any Town or City; otherwise to be dropt.[21]

Regarding some of the tactics in use at this period for the cavalry armed with arquebuse or carbine, we note the following:

Files firing in the Front. . . . The right hand File and the left hand File March some distance before the head of the Troop, and Rank themselves to the right and left inward, and so Present and Give fire; which being performed, let them wheel off to the right and left outwards into the Reer of their first Station, and so set themselves in their respective places even with the remainder of the Body, leaving distance for every Rank to march into his proper place, after they have fired over. . . .

I shall now demonstrate one platforme of firing by Rank. . . . But in firing by Rank, observe the first Rank may advance upon a large Trot, Gallop, or Carrere, as Command is given between thirty or fourty paces from the Body. The first Rank having fired wheels off to the left (if occasion will permit) and falls into the Reer; and immediately upon the wheeling off of the first Rank, the second advanceth according to Command and fireth, and so the third.[22]

Turning our attention to the continent, we learn that in the reign of Frederick William of Prussia (father of Frederick the Great),

His cavalry were well drilled to fire in line, both on foot and on horseback: nothing was done to make them formidable in close combat; they charged at a walk or a trot.[23]

And finally, we present several illustrations of cavalry action from the Napoleonic period, in which the muzzle-loading flintlock was still standard equipment as the cavalry firearm. The first dates from the campaign of 1813 and concerns an action between the French and the Cossacks:

The French advanced at a trot, and, to prevent the Russians getting in betwixt the squadrons, they closed up and bore right down on the centre of our line, which naturally opened out; the Cossacks attacking the flank and rear of the column. The French, having no one in front to oppose them, halted, whilst their tormenters kept spearing the flank files and *firing* into the mass, which soon got into complete confusion and could undertake no evolution of any sort. The Cossacks, though they never attempted to disperse the mass by a dash at them, still, conscious of their superiority in riding, *continued to shoot* and spear them, executing partial charges when opportunity offered. Meanwhile the flank files

[21] *Ibid.*, pp. 13–14.
[22] *Ibid.*, pp. 22–23.
[23] Nolan, 1854, p. 30.

of the French faced outwards and unslung their carabines, and, thus formed in square, they *kept up an irregular fusillade for about half an hour*.[24]

And another engagement in which

The French completed their movements whilst the Cossacks were forming up; they were formed in one line, en muraille, with a small reserve in rear. The Cossacks fell on, and were received with a discharge of carabines; the French did not draw swords. Their fire, at first, sent the Russians to the right about; and, whilst they were reforming, the enemy wheeled into column and opened out, so as to get their intervals wheeled again into line.[25]

As a concluding remark, it should also be noted that a rather long-barreled, flintlock muzzle-loader formed an integral part of the equipment used by the cavalry of tribal Arabia and North Africa in the 19th and even 20th centuries.

[24] *Ibid.*, p. 82. Italics FRS.
[25] *Ibid.*, pp. 83–84.

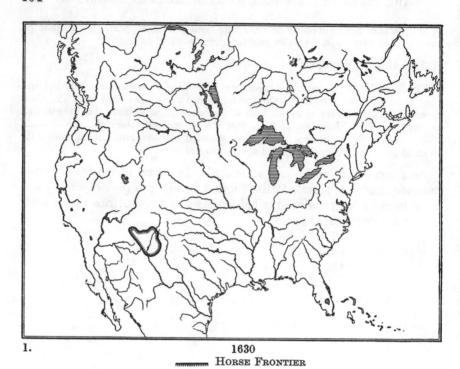

1.
1630
〰〰〰 HORSE FRONTIER

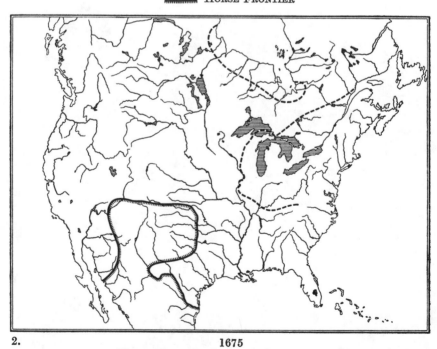

2.
1675
〰〰〰 HORSE FRONTIER   ------ GUN FRONTIER

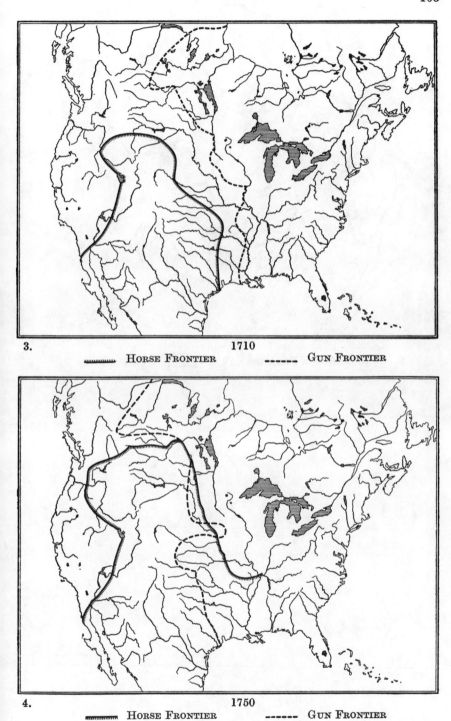

3.   1710

━━━━━━━ Horse Frontier   ------ Gun Frontier

4.   1750

━━━━━━━ Horse Frontier   ------ Gun Frontier

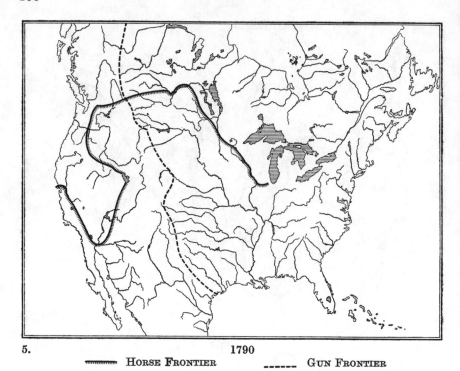

5.   1790

━━━━━━━ Horse Frontier   ------ Gun Frontier

BIBLIOGRAPHY

BANDELIER, A. F. A. AND HACKETT, C. W.
  1937. *Historical Documents Relating to New Mexico, Nueva Vizcaya, and Approaches Thereto, to 1773.* Coll. by A. F. A. Bandelier and ed. by C. W. Hackett. Vol. 3, Washington, D. C.
BARWICK, HUMPHREY
  1580-90. *A Breefe Discourse, Concerning the force and effect of all manuall weapons of fire, and the disability of the Long Bowe or Archery, in respect of others of greater force now in use.* London.
BENEDICT, RUTH
  1922. "The Vision in Plains Culture." *American Anthropologist*, New Series, Vol. 24.
  1934. *Patterns of Culture.* Boston and New York.
BLAIR, E. H.
  1911. *The Indian Tribes of the Upper Mississippi Valley and the Region of the Great Lakes.* 2 Vols. Cleveland.
BOLTON, H. E.
  1911. "The Jumano Indians in Texas, 1650-1771." *The Quarterly of the Texas State Historical Association*, Vol. 15.
  1914. *Athanase de Mezieres and the Louisiana-Texas Frontier, 1768-1780.* 2 Vols. Cleveland.
  1915. *Texas in the Middle 18th Century.* California University Publications in History. Vol. 3. Berkeley.
  1916. (ed.) *Spanish Exploration in the Southwest, 1542-1706.* New York.
BURPEE, L. J.
  1907. (ed.) *The Journal of Anthony Hendry, 1754-55.* Royal Society of Canada, Proceedings and Transactions, Third Series, Vol. 1. Ottawa.
  1909. (ed.) *Matthew Cocking's Journal.* Royal Society of Canada, Proceedings and Transactions, Third Series, Vol. 2. Ottawa.
  1927. (ed.) *Journals and Letters of Pierre Gautier de Varennes de la Verendry and his Sons.* The Champlain Society, Vol. 16. Toronto.
CARROLL, H. B. AND HAGGARD, J. V.
  1942. (trans. and ed.) *Three New Mexico Chronicles.* The Quivira Society, Albuquerque.
CLEMENTS, F. E. AND SHELFORD, V. E.
  1939. *Bio-Ecology.* New York and London.
CORRESPONDENCE GÉNÉRALE LOUISIANE
  1716. in *Archives du Ministere des Colonies.* Serie C 13. Vol. 4. Paris (Transcript in *Mississippi Provincial Archives, French Dominion.* Vol. 7, unpublished Ms. in Department of Archives and History, State of Mississippi).
COUES, E.
  1897. (ed.) *New Light on the Early History of the Greater Northwest, Henry-Thompson Journals.* 2 Vols. New York.
CURTIS, F. S., JR.
  1927. "Spanish Arms and Armor in the Southwest," *New Mexico Historical Review*, Vol. 2.

DENHARDT, R. M.
    1947.   *The Horse of the Americas*. Norman, Oklahoma.
DOBRIZHOFFER, MARTIN
    1822.   *An Account of the Abipones, an Equestrian People of Paraguay.*
            Vol. 2. London.
DODGE, COLONEL R. I.
    1882.   *Our Wild Indians*. Hartford and Chicago.
DUNN, J. P.
    1905.   *Indiana*. Boston and New York.
DUNN, W. E.
    1910–11.   "Apache Relations in Texas, 1718–1750," *Quarterly of the Texas
               State Historical Association*, Vol. 14.
ESPINOSA, J. MANUEL
    1942.   *Crusaders of the Rio Grande*. Chicago.
FLETCHER, ALICE C. AND LA FLESCHE, FRANCIS
    1905–06.   *The Omaha Tribe*. Annual Report of the Bureau of American
               Ethnology, Vol. 27. Washington, D. C.
FRANKLIN, JOHN
    1823.   *Narrative of a Journey to the Shores of the Polar Sea in the Years 1819,
            20, 21 and 22*. London.
FRENCH, B. F.
    1851.   *Historical Collections of Louisiana*. Vol. 3. New York.
    1852.   *Historical Collections of Louisiana*. Vol. 4. New York.
GLUCKMAN, Col. ARCADI
    1948.   *United States Muskets, Rifles, and Carbines*. Buffalo.
GOLDFRANK, ESTHER S.
    1943.   "Historic Change and Social Character: A Study of the Teton-
            Dakota," *American Anthropologist*, New Series, Vol. 45.
HAINES, FRANCIS
    1938a.   "Where did the Plains Indians get their Horses," *American Anthro-
             pologist*, New Series, Vol. 40.
    1938b.   "The Northward Spread of Horses among the Plains Indians,"
             American Anthropologist, New Series, Vol. 40.
HAINES, HELEN
    1891. *History of New Mexico*. New York.
HAMILTON, J. C.
    1898.   "The Panis—an Historical Outline of Canadian Indian Slavery in
            the Eighteenth Century," *Proceedings of the Royal Canadian In-
            stitute*, New Series, Vol. 1. Toronto.
HAMMOND, G. P. and Rey, Agapito
    1927.   (trans. and ed.) *The Gallegos Relation of the Rodriguez Expedition to
            New Mexico*. Historical Society of New Mexico Publications in His-
            tory, Vol. 4, Santa Fe.
HILL, W. W.
    1936. *Navajo Warfare*, Yale University Publications in Anthropology,
          No. 5. New Haven.
HODGE, F. W.
    1907.   (ed.) *Spanish Explorers in the Southern United States, 1528–43.*
            Original Narratives of Early American History, Vol. 2, New York.
    1945.   (ed.) *Fray Alonso de Benavides' Revised Memorial of 1634*. Albu-
            querque.
HORNADAY, W. T.
    1887.   "The Extermination of the American Bison," *Smithsonian Institution
            Annual Report*, Pt. 2. Washington D. C.

HOUGH, WALTER
1895. "Primitive American Armor," *Annual Report of the Board of Regents of the Smithsonian Institution, 1893*. Washington, D. C.
HYDE, GEORGE E.
1933. *The Early Blackfeet and their Neighbors*. Denver.
1937. *Red Cloud's Folk*. Norman, Oklahoma.
INNIS, H. A.
1930a. *Peter Pond, Fur Trader and Adventurer*. Toronto.
1930b. *The Fur Trade in Canada*. New Haven and London.
JABLOW, JOSEPH
1951. *The Cheyenne in Plains Indian Trade Relations, 1795–1840*. Monographs of the American Ethnological Society. No. XIX. New York.
"J. V."
1858. "De l'Esclavage en Canada." *Memoires de la Societé Historique de Montreal*. Vols. 1–5.
KROEBER, A. L.
1947. *Cultural and Natural Areas of Native North America*. Berkeley.
LA HONTAN, Baron de
1905. *New Voyages to North America*. ed. by R. G. Thwaites. 2 Vols. Chicago.
LAUBER, A. W.
1913. *Indian Slavery in Colonial Times Within the Present Limits of the United States*. New York.
LENZ, E. C.
1944. *Muzzle Flashes*. Huntington, West Virginia.
LESSER, ALEXANDER
1933. *The Pawnee Ghost Dance Hand Game*. Columbia University Contributions to Anthropology, Vol. 16. New York.
LEWIS, ANNA
1924. "La Harpe's First Expedition in Oklahoma," *Chronicles of Oklahoma*. Vol. 2.
LEWIS AND CLARK
1904–05. *Original Journals of the Lewis and Clark Expedition, 1804–1806*. ed. by R. G. Thwaites. 8 Vols. New York.
LEWIS, OSCAR
1942. *The Effects of White Contact upon Blackfoot Culture*. Monographs of the American Ethnological Society, No. VI. New York.
LINTON, RALPH
1936. *The Study of Man*. New York and London.
LOWIE, R. H.
1924. "Shoshonean Ethnography," *Anthropological Papers of the American Museum of Natural History*. Vol. 20. New York.
MACKENZIE, ALEXANDER
1902. *Voyages from Montreal through the Continent of North America to the Frozen and Pacific Oceans in 1789 and 1793*. 2 Vols. New York.
MACLEOD, WILLIAM CRISTIE
1928. *The American Indian Frontier*. London and New York.
MANDELBAUM, D. G.
1940. *The Plains Cree*. Anthropological Papers of the American Museum of Natural History. Vol. 37. New York.
MARGRY, PIERRE
1879–88. *Découvertes et établissements des français dans l'ouest et dans le sud de l'Amerique Septentrionale (1614–1754)*. Impr. D. Jouaust. 6 Vols. Paris.

MARQUIS, THOMAS B.
    1928.   (ed.) *Memoirs of a White Crow Indian.* New York and London.
MARTIN, P. S., Quimby, G. I., and Collier, Donald
    1947.   *Indians Before Columbus.* Chicago.
MISHKIN, BERNARD
    1940.   *Rank and Warfare Among the Plains Indians.* Monographs of the
            American Ethnological Society, No. III. New York.
MOONEY, JAMES
    1895–96. "Calendar History of the Kiowa Indians," *Annual Report
            of the Bureau of American Ethnology,* Vol. 17, Pt. 1. Washington,
            D. C.
MORICE, A. G.
    1889–90. "The Western Denes," *Proceedings of the Canadian Institute.*
            Third Series, Vol. 7. Toronto.
NOLAN, CAPT. L. E.
    1854.   *Cavalry, Its History and Tactics.* London.
PAREDES, FRAY ALONSO DE
    1686.   "Utiles y curiosas noticias del Nuevo-Mexico, Cibola y otras naciones
            confinantes", in *Documentos para la Historia de Mexico.* Third Series,
            Vol. 1, Pt. 4, pp. 209–225. Mexico, 1856.
PARSONS, JOHN E.
    1952.   "Gunmakers for the American Fur Company." *The New York His-
            torical Society Quarterly,* Vol. 36. New York.
RADISSON, PIERRE ESPRIT
    1885.   *Voyages of Peter Esprit Radisson.* Publications of the Prince Society,
            Vol. 16, Boston.
RANDS, ROBERT L.
    1950.   *A Chart of Plains Populations.* Unpublished Ms., Dept. of Anthropo-
            logy, Columbia University.
RECOPILACION DE LEYAS DE LOS REYNOS DE LAS INDIAS
    1943.   Madrid.
RUSSELL, FRANK
    1903.   "Pima Annals," *American Anthropologist,* New Series, Vol. 5.
SALMERON, FRAY GERONIMO DE ZARATE
    1626.   Quoted by Niel, Padre Juan Amando, 1718, and republished in
            Documentos para la Historiade Mexico. Third series, Vol. 1, Pt. 4,
            pp. 56–112. Mexico, 1856.
SCHOLES, F. V.
    1935.   "Civil Government and Society in New Mexico in the Seventeenth
            Century," *New Mexico Historical Review,* Vol. 10.
SCHULTZ, J. W.
    1907.   *My Life as an Indian.* New York.
SECOY, FRANK R.
    1951.   "The Identity of the 'Paduca': an, Ethno-historical Analysis,"
            American Anthropologist. Vol. 53.
SMITH, MARIAN W.
    1938.   "The War Complex of the Plains Indians," *Proceedings of the
            American Philosophical Society,* Vol. 78. Philadelphia.
SMITH, T. W.
    1896–98. "The Slave in Canada," *Nova Scotia Historical Society, Reports,*
            Vol. 10. Halifax, N. S.
SOPER, J. D.
    1941.   "History, Range, and Homelife of the Northern Bison," *Ecological
            Monographs,* Vol. 1.

SPIER, LESLIE
1921. "The Sun Dance of the Plains Indians; Its Development and Diffusion," *Anthropological Papers of the American Museum of Natural History*, Vol. 16. New York.

STRONG, WM. DUNCAN
1935. *An Introduction to Nebraska Archaeology*, Smithsonian Miscellaneous Collections, Vol. 93, No. 10. Washington, D. C.
1936. "Anthropological Theory and Archaeological Fact," in *Essays in Honor of Alfred Louis Kroeber*, ed. by R. H. Lowie. Berkeley.
1940. "From History to Prehistory in the Northern Great Plains," *Smithsonian Miscellaneous Collections*, Vol. 100, Washington, D. C.

SURREY, N. M. M.
1916. *The Commerce of Louisiana During the French Regime, 1699–1763*. New York.

THOMAS, A. B.
1924. "The Massacre of the Villasur Expedition," *Nebraska History Magazine*, Vol. 7.
1929. "San Carlos, A Comanche Pueblo on the Arkansas R., 1787," *Colorado Magazine*, Vol. 6.
1935. (trans. and ed.) *After Coronado, Spanish Exploration Northeast of New Mexico, 1696–1727, Documents from the Archives of Spain, Mexico, and New Mexico*. Norman, Oklahoma.

TYRELL, J. B.
1916. (ed.) *David Thompson's Narrative of his Explorations in Western America, 1784–1812*. The Champlain Society Publications, Vol. 12. Toronto.
1934. (ed.) *Journals of Samuel Hearne and Philip Turnor*. The Champlain Society Publications, Vol. 21. Toronto.

UMFREVILLE
1790. *The Fur Trade of Hudson's Bay*. London.

VENN, THOMAS
1672. *Military and Maritime Discipline*. London.

WEDEL, WALDO R.
1938. "Hopewellian Remains near Kansas City, Missouri," *Proceedings of the U.S. National Museum*, LXXXVI. Washington, D. C.
1940. "Culture Sequences in the Central Great Plains," in *Essays in Historical Anthropology of North America*. Smithsonian Miscellaneous Collections, Vol. 100. Washington, D. C.
1941. "Environment and Native Subsistence Economies in the Central Great Plains." *Smithsonian Miscellaneous Collections*, Vol. 101, No. 3. Washington, D. C.
1943. "Archaeological Investigations in Platte and Clay Counties, Missouri," *U.S. National Museum*, Bull. 183. Washington, D. C.

WINSHIP, G. P.
1892–93. "The Coronado Expedition, 1540–42," *Annual Reports of the Bureau of American Ethnology*, Vol. 14, Pt. 1. Washington, D. C.

WISCONSIN HISTORICAL COLLECTIONS
1857. Vol. 3.
1908. Vol. 18. ed. by R. G. Thwaites.
1910. Vol. 19. ed. by R. G. Thwaites.

WISSLER, CLARK
1910. "Material Culture of the Blackfoot Indians," *Anthropological Papers of the American Museum of Natural History*, Vol. 5. New York.

1911.   (ed.) "Societies of the Plains Indians," *Anthropological Papers of the American Museum of Natural History*, Vol. 7. New York.

1912.   "Societies and Ceremonial Associations in the Oglala Division of the Teton-Dakota," *Anthropological Papers of the American Museum of Natural History*, Vol. 11. New York.

1914.   "The Influence of the Horse in the Development of Plains Culture," *American Anthropologist*, New Series, Vol. 16.

1915 a. "Material Cultures of the North American Indians," in *Anthropology in North America* by Franz Boas et al. New York.

1915 b. "Riding Gear of the North American Indians," *Anthropological Papers of the American Museum of Natural History*, Vol. 17. New York.

1926.   *The Relation of Nature to Man in Aboriginal America*. New York and London.

WORCESTER, D. E.

1944.   "The Spread of Spanish Horses in the Southwest," *New Mexico Historical Review*, Vol. 19.

Finishing the Race at 10 P.M.1975

Michigan Cross Country - 1976
By Frank Howard Hall

With many months of thinking and preparing, I figured I was ready for our cross country run. I had thought about my dogs—they were conditioned for speed while all my buddies had had several dry runs with loaded sleds at different races.

In the past year I had designed a different type of sled for cross-country. Several ended up used by various drivers in the race. They had two inch runners, a six-foot bed (including front bow) long enough to sleep in. This worked super for me.

I carried all the mandatory equipment as required in the rules.

I was rather concerned with the starting speed that my team had. With loaded sled, running twelve dogs, we made the first 25 miles in just under two hours. The dogs finally settled down to a slower pace which was what I wanted. The team has to set its own pace. My starting time was 1:20 P.M. By 7:40 P.M. I had gone 54 miles.

The last couple hours of the first day and all the second day was in a howling blizzard off Lake Superior. The only let-up was in heavy timber. Going across open areas with the trail blown shut was rather traumatic. Some advice right here might be in order. Should you go off the trail with bad conditions or at night, turn around and go back to the trail. This is when a fellow could get into serious trouble. One of our guys this year got lost and it was a lesson for all of us. This is extremely remote country up in northern Michigan. There could be times when it would be hard for a rescue team to know where to start looking for a lost driver. However, with using some horse sense, he could be found before getting into real bad trouble.

I made camps rather simple, slept in the sled, and set up no tent. I fed my dogs three times a day: meatballs rolled in dog food which I had made ahead of time, frozen, and stored in a plastic bag with just enough for the whole team in one bag.

Feeding dogs in this manner kept their spirits and energy

up. I couldn't get the dogs to drink so I let them eat snow for moisture intake. You get a bit dehydrated yourself. Soups and milk are good except you have to keep thawing out freezable items.

Our trails were as good as could ever be – packed snowmobile trails

We had 42 inches of snow on the level. The hardest part of all was getting off a plowed road, up over a steep snow bank, and back on the trail. This was my greatest concern – hoping there would be someone available to help at these spots. In most cases, it worked out.

We had as great a variety of trails as there could be anywhere except we had no mountains in the distance or long downhill runs.

The dogs learned quickly to take advantage of resting. In speed races, I have observed and experienced the fact that many teams are not too eager to get under motion on that third day of a three day race. In cross country running, I experienced this same thing. Let's say that you stop on the trail for a breather. After a few minutes, the whole team is lying down. When you are ready to go, you step on the runners and give the command. Nothing happens! Some dogs don't even look up at you. What do you do? I walked toward the leaders and started picking them up, making them stand, talking gay all the time. When I got the whole team on its feet, I got back on the runners, pulled the hook, and gave a very excited command. Off they go!

It might take a mile for the team to really get with it. The start in the morning might take five miles for the whole team to really get under motion. I never had to pick them up in the morning. They were always ready to go. This is a totally different dimension than s speed race. A tugline might go slack for a while. The dog is just relaxing and readjusting. If he does this too long, stop the team. You might end up letting him ride a while. Don't be too disturbed. This is part of the game.

On one occasion, night and a check point were

approaching. We had nearly 70 miles under the runners since morning. I registered at the checkpoint and rested the dogs for about an hour. I knew the next 20 miles I couldn't get off the trail, the moon was half out making visibility very good; therefore, I wanted to continue on. If you have never driven your team at night, you are missing a treat. They are more alert, more aggressive, and more eager even when tired. It ended up being a very delightful memory in my mushing experience. The temperature was about 10 above 0, with ghostly figures ahead of my sled, ears up, and all working beautifully. A slight breeze was in my face, a few clouds filtered across the moon. This was dog mushing magnifico!

At 10:45 I came upon my campsite of two nights before (the trail back-tracked in several places.) The dogs sensed they were home for the night. I secured the sled, picketed and fed the dogs, ate, and climbed into my sleeping bag. All this was done in less than 30 minutes. I had gone nearly 90 miles that day.

This was an interesting place to camp. It was under a big pine tree but across the trail (a road in summer) stood a monument in memory of a couple who had frozen to death a few years before at this very spot. I knew this but I had everything under control. As I slept, all was well. I was only 25 miles from the finish line. I would cross it by noon the next day.

There wasn't a loser in our whole group. On the trail, we cheered each other on. We always stopped and talked when passing or meeting head-on. There was a great feeling of respect toward each other. We faced and endured every kind of weather; rain, blizzard, sleet, dark days, beautiful sunny days, dark nights, and moonlit nights. We made it, but it wasn't easy.

My advice is to train your team for power and get yourself in condition. Camp out as often as you can – even in mild weather. If you prepare your dogs and yourself, when winter comes you can do your thing – relaxed – without the pressure of speed racing. My guess is you'll like it!